©Master Key
to the
GRE

Volume 1

Arithmetic &
"Plan B" Strategies

Repasar

1: 3 ultimas
2: 4/7/9/18/26/27/28
3: 4/7/17/20/24/23/29

Made by
Sherpa Pre

D1530664

Master Key to the GRE: Arithmetic & "Plan B" Strategies.

ISBN: 978-0-9966225-4-7

Register Your Book!

To access the online videos that come with this book, please go to:

www.SherpaPrep.com/Activate

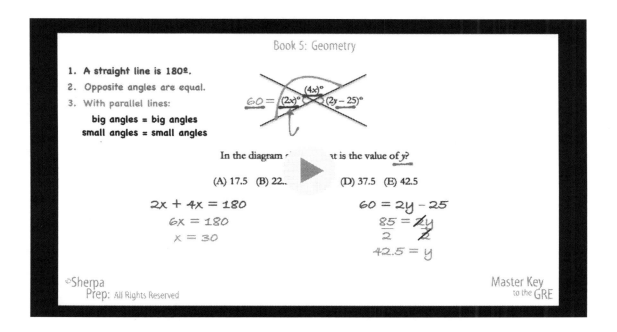

When registering:

Be sure to provide the **same** last name and shipping address that you used to purchase this book or to enroll in your GRE course with Sherpa Prep!

Register @ www.SherpaPrep.com/Activate

Master Key by
Sherpa Prep

Dear Student,

Thank you for purchasing Sherpa Prep's guide to <u>Arithmetic & "Plan B" Strategies</u>. We know that preparing for the GRE can be a grueling and intimidating process. The fact that you've chosen us to assist you is deeply appreciated.

This series of books is the culmination of nearly three decades of experience teaching the GRE on a daily basis. We think you'll find that experience and expertise reflected in the pages that follow.

As with any undertaking of this size, there are a number of people who deserve special recognition. First among them is Nasheed Amin, who critiqued <u>Master Key to the GRE</u> in its entirety and whose insightful recommendations significantly enhanced all five volumes. We would also like to recognize the contributions of Seth Alcorn, Shawn Magnuson, Bronwyn Bruton, and Jessica Rider Amin. Without their assistance, this project would not have been possible. Finally, we would like to extend our gratitude to the students and instructors of Sherpa Prep, whose feedback, questions, and experiences lie at the heart of these materials.

Good luck with your preparation! If we can be of further assistance, please reach out to us at **jay@sherpaprep.com** or **nafeez@sherpaprep.com**. We'd love to hear from you.

On behalf of everyone at Sherpa Prep,

Jay

Nafeez

Jay Friedman
Founder
Sherpa Prep

Nafeez Amin
President
Sherpa Prep

Table of Contents

Volume 1

Arithmetic & "Plan B" Strategies

Chapter 1

Introduction to the GRE

Introduction

To be discussed:

Master Key to the GRE

Get a sense of how to use our books, how to study properly for the GRE, and how to access our online video content.

1 Choosing the Right Guide	**4** Proper Study Habits
2 Why Master Key is Special	**5** The App
3 How to Use Our Guides	**6** Register Your Book!

The Structure & Scoring System

Read about the structure and scoring system of the GRE. Learn how to sign up for the exam and report your scores.

7 The Structure of the GRE	**9** Registering for the GRE
8 The Scoring System	**10** Reporting & Canceling Scores

Navigating the Exam

Get an in-depth sense of how the GRE's scoring system works and what you can do to maximize your performance on test day.

11 How the Exam Works	**13** Strategy & Time Management
12 The Scoring Algorithm	**14** Practice Tests

Intro to Quantitative Reasoning

Before you get started, educate yourself about the sort of math you'll find on the GRE and the four ways in which the exam formats its math questions.

15 Content Overview	**18** Numeric Entry Questions
16 Problem Solving Questions	**19** Quantitative Comparisons
17 "Select One or More" Questions	**20** Before You Get Started

Master Key to the GRE

(1) Choosing the Right Guide – If you're like most people preparing to take the GRE, you probably have little sense of what differentiates one GRE guide from another.

• You may think that all GRE guides are more or less the same, or that the guides you see in bookstores are the most comprehensive on the market.

> ➤ The basic story is that most guides fall into one of two categories: "strategy-based" or "content-based".

• **The guides that you find in bookstores are almost always strategy-based**. In general, strategy-based guides provide:

1. A brief discussion of each question type that you find on the GRE.
2. A small set of suggestions for approaching these question types.
3. A collection of one hundred or so practice questions with some brief solutions.

• You also tend to find instructions on how to register for the GRE and report your scores; advice for the test day experience; and a few appendices that review vocabulary and elementary math principles.

> ➤ You won't find a lot of "know-how", however, in strategy-based guides. **The focus of such books is test-taking advice, not education**.

• The latest "premier" guide of one well-known test-prep provider, for example, devotes just nineteen pages to explaining math concepts.

• This said, you will find some useful ideas for taking the exam strategically, among them: ways to use the answer choices to your advantage; advice on how to pace yourself; and recommendations on how to read.

> ➤ In our experience, learning these sorts of strategies is helpful for most test-takers. Unfortunately, **they will not help you attain a strong GRE score, on their own**.

• If you do not know how to solve the problems you find on your exam, you will not do well, regardless of how well you can eliminate irrational answers, pace yourself, or otherwise "game" the exam.

> ➤ In contrast, **content-based guides teach the "know-how" you need** to solve exam questions without guessing.

• Such guides generally devote several pages of discussion to most of the major topics tested by the GRE.

• At the end of each discussion, you tend to find a set of section-ending exercises that allow you to practice what you've studied. As a result, content-based guides almost always have far more practice questions than their strategy-based counterparts.

> ➤ In our view, **this sort of approach is critical to success on the GRE**. It may not be the only thing you need to succeed, but it is the most important.

• Think about it logically for a moment. Is there any other exam you would dare take without learning its content beforehand?

• Of course not. Yet students regularly "prep" for the GRE using books that do not review the content of the exam. It takes years to graduate from college, and some admissions committees weigh GRE scores more heavily than grade point averages. Isn't an exam that means so much worth preparing for properly?

> ➤ Unfortunately, there a number of drawbacks to the content-based guides currently available for the GRE.

• For starters, **these guides almost always ignore the tactics recommended by strategy-based guides**, tactics that we believe are an asset to any test taker.

• What's more, such guides rarely tell you how frequently a particular topic is tested. Knowing which topics to study is important if you only have limited time to prepare for the GRE!

> ➤ Most importantly, none of the guides actually teach you EVERYTHING tested by the GRE.

• While most cover the major topics found on a typical exam, **none cover the vast array of rare and advanced concepts that you need to grasp if you're hoping to score <u>above</u> the 90th percentile.**

(2) Why Master Key Is Special – <u>Master Key to the GRE</u> is the only guide to the GRE that will teach you everything you need to attain a perfect score.

• Whether you're looking for help with advanced concepts, or are starting from scratch, our materials will have what you need.

> ➤ **We start by assuming you know NOTHING.** Everything is laid out for you as if you haven't done math in years.

• Each chapter focuses on a specific topic, such as Fractions, Rates, or Triangles, and opens with a thorough discussion of its simplest, most fundamental concepts.

• Bit by bit, we gradually explore ALL the wrinkles associated with that topic, so that you can solve problems involving sophisticated nuances, not just easy problems.

> ➤ At the ends of our chapters, you'll find a treatment of **every RARE and ADVANCED concept tested by the GRE.**

• You won't find these topics discussed anywhere else. <u>Master Key to the GRE</u> is the only resource that covers them.

• We know that some of you only need help solving the most difficult questions — the questions that determine who scores ABOVE the 90th percentile. We've made sure that our guides teach <u>everything</u>, so that students in your position get all the support they need.

> ➤ To keep things simple, we discuss math in **language that's EASY to understand** and focus on **SMART strategies for every level of material.**

• In writing <u>Master Key to the GRE</u>, we were determined to make our guides helpful for everyone, not just math geeks.

• We are GRE specialists who have spent our entire professional careers making math ACCESSIBLE to students who hate it. **These books are the culmination of over three decades of daily classroom instruction.** No matter how difficult a topic may be, we walk you through each concept, step by step, to ensure that everything makes sense.

> ➤ Along the way, **we sprinkle in hundreds of SHORTCUTS and TRICKS** that you won't find in any other guide.

• We know that TIME is a major concern for many test-takers, so we've included every time-saving strategy out there to help you "beat the clock".

Chapter 1: Introduction

- We don't care how well you think you know math. These shortcuts will save you valuable minutes, no matter what your current skill level may be.

  ➤ To complement our content-oriented approach, the first volume of <u>Master Key to the GRE</u> devotes **an entire chapter to something we call "Plan B" strategies**.

- A "Plan B" strategy is a strategy that can help you deduce a correct answer when you don't know how to solve a problem.

- Such "tricks of the trade" are sometimes encountered in mainstream strategy-based guides. No other guide, however, features a collection like the one we've put together here. We've got all of the tricks, not just a few.

  ➤ We also complement our content-oriented approach by telling you **how FREQUENTLY the GRE tests every concept** — something no other guide does.

- We know that most people don't have the time to study everything and aren't looking for a perfect score — just a score that's good enough to get them into the school of their choice.

- So, we let you know which topics are <u>commonly tested</u> and which ones are not so that you can determine for yourself which topics are worth your time.

  ➤ Additionally, **we organize our discussions by level of DIFFICULTY**, as well as by topic.

- As we see it, test-takers deserve to know which topics they need to master in order to get elite scores and which topics they can afford to skip if they're only looking for above average scores.

- Our hope is that by organizing our material in this way, you'll be able to limit your efforts to material that is right for you.

  ➤ In total, <u>Master Key to the GRE</u> includes **nearly ONE THOUSAND practice questions**. That's more than any other resource out there.

- Like our teaching sections, our practice questions are sorted by difficulty, as well as by topic, so that you can focus on any level of material and on any topic that you like.

- Moreover, nearly a quarter of these questions involve the most rare or advanced topics tested by the GRE. So if you're looking for a lot of help with diabolical fare, you'll find it here.

➤ Most of the solutions to these questions come in the form of **ANIMATED VIDEOS, which you can play on any computer, tablet, or smart phone**.

• We understand that the short, written explanations found in other GRE handbooks are often insufficient for students who find math challenging.

• By providing you with video solutions, we are able to talk you through our practice problems, every step of the way, so that you can follow along easily and see where your solution went wrong.

➤ In many cases, you'll find that our animated videos discuss **multiple ways to solve a question**.

• In math, there is often more than one way to solve a problem. Not all of these approaches, however, are equally efficient.

• Our videos discuss the best of these approaches to ensure that you're exposed to a solution that's not only fast and simple, but also works well with your way of thinking.

➤ We know that <u>Master Key to the GRE</u> is the most expensive GRE guide on the market.

• It's anywhere from $60 to $100 dollars more expensive than most of the alternatives out there. That's a lot of money.

• But let us ask you this. Which would rather have: an extra $60 to $100 dollars or the GRE scores that you need?

➤ Remember, it took you years to graduate from college, and many admissions committees weigh GRE scores more heavily than your grade point average.

• Isn't an exam that means so much worth the cost of a college textbook? Of course it is.

• If you're still not certain, **we encourage you to compare our materials to anything else** that you can find. Whether you're looking for help with advanced material or something a little less extreme, we have no doubt that you'll see why <u>Master Key to the GRE</u> is worth the difference.

Chapter 1: Introduction

(3) How to Use Our Guides – As mentioned, <u>Master Key to the GRE</u> has been designed to help you solve EVERY question on the GRE.

• It explains ALL of the TOUGH concepts that no other GRE prep book attempts to cover, not just the easy ones.

> ➤ Depending on your goals, however, you may NOT need to master everything. Not every program requires a perfect score. In fact, most don't require anything close.

• If you've yet to do so, we strongly encourage you to contact the programs you're interested in to see what sort of scores they require.

• Knowing "how high" to set the bar will give you a sense of whether you need to cover everything or just the core material. (Remember, we'll tell you how frequently each topic is tested!)

> ➤ Every volume of <u>Master Key to the GRE</u> has been designed to help someone starting from SCRATCH to build, step by step, to the most challenging material.

• Thus, Chapter 1 is intended to precede Chapter 2, and the same is true for each volume: <u>Arithmetic & "Plan B" Strategies</u> (Vol. 1) is intended to precede <u>Number Properties & Algebra</u> (Vol. 2).

• The chapters, however, are largely independent of one another, as are the books, so you're welcome to skip around if you only need help with a few key topics or are short on time.

> ➤ As you study, bear in mind that you DON'T have to master one topic before studying another.

• If you have a hard time with something, put it aside for a day or two. It can take one or two "exposures" for a concept to "click" – especially if it's new or tricky.

• You also don't need to solve all 1,000 of our practice problems. If you're comfortable with a topic, feel free to skip the questions marked "fundamental" to save time.

> ➤ Finally, remember that our ADVANCED materials are intended for students in need of PERFECT scores.

• If that's not you, don't waste your time! Questions involving advanced topics are generally rare for the GRE, so if you'd be thrilled with a score around the 90th percentile, you're more likely to achieve it by focusing on questions and materials involving core concepts.

(4) Proper Study Habits – Whatever your goals may be for the GRE, it's important that you work consistently.

• Studying a little EVERY DAY is the best way to retain what you're learning and to avoid the burn out that comes with studying too intensely for too long.

> ➤ In a perfect world, we'd have you study about an hour a day during the workweek and one to two hours a day on the weekends.

• Unfortunately, we know that such a schedule is unrealistic for some people. If you can't find an hour each day, at least DO SOMETHING!

• Even 5 minutes a day can help you stave off rust and prevent the cycle of guilt and procrastination that comes from not studying.

> ➤ If you can, do your best to AVOID CRAMMING. Much of what you'll be studying is boring and technical. It will take "elbow grease" to master.

• We truly question how much of this information can be absorbed in a few short weeks or in study sessions that last three or four hours.

• In our experience, most students who do too much too rapidly either burnout or fail to absorb the material properly.

> ➤ To avoid "study fatigue", SWITCH things up. Spend part of each day studying for the math portion of the exam and part for the verbal portion.

• And do your best to incorporate at least part of your study routine into your daily life.

• If you can study 30 minutes out of every lunch break and a few minutes out of every snack break, we think you'll find that you have more time to prepare than you might believe. We also think you'll find the shorter study sessions more beneficial.

> ➤ As you study, be sure to bear in mind that QUALITY is just as important as QUANTITY.

• Many test-takers believe that the key to success is to work through thousands of practice questions and to take dozens of exams. This simply isn't true.

- While working through practice questions and taking exams are important parts of preparing for the GRE, doing so does not mean that you are LEARNING the material.

  ➤ It is equally important that you LEARN from your MISTAKES. Whenever you miss a practice question, be sure to watch the video explanation that we've provided.

- Then, redo the problem yourself. Once you feel that you've "got it", come back to the problem two days later.

- If you still get it wrong, add the problem to your "LOG of ERRORS" and redo it every few weeks. Keeping track of tricky problems and redoing them MORE THAN ONCE is a great way to learn from your mistakes and to avoid similar difficulties on your actual exam.

  ➤ As you prepare, keep the REAL exam in mind. The GRE tests your ability to recognize concepts under TIMED conditions. Your study habits should reflect this.

- If it takes you 3 minutes to solve a problem, you may as well have missed that problem. 3 minutes is too much time to spend on a problem during an actual exam. Be sure to watch the video solutions for such problems and to redo them until you can solve them quickly.

- Likewise, bear in mind that you will take the GRE on a COMPUTER, unless you opt to take the paper-based version that is administered only three times a year.

  ➤ So adopt GOOD HABITS now. Whenever you practice, avoid doing things you can't do on a computer, such as writing atop problems or underlining key words.

- And make a NOTECARD whenever you learn something. The cards don't have to be complicated – even a sample problem that illustrates the concept will do.

- As your studying progresses, it can be easy to forget concepts that you learned at the beginning of your preparation. Notecards will help you retain what you've learned and make it easy for you to review that material whenever you have a few, spare minutes.

  ➤ Finally, do your best to keep your emotions in check. It's easy to become overconfident when a practice exam goes well or to get down when one goes poorly.

- The GRE is a tough exam and improvement, for most students, takes time.

- In our experience, however, test-takers who prepare like PROFESSIONALS — who keep an even keel, who put in the time to do their assignments properly, and who commit to identifying their weaknesses and improving them – ALWAYS achieve their goals in the end.

(5) The App – <u>Master Key to the GRE</u> is available in print through Amazon or through our website at **www.sherpaprep.com/masterkey**.

• It's also available as an app for iPhones and iPads through Apple's App Store under the title <u>GRE Math by Sherpa Prep</u>.

➢ Like the printed edition, the app comes with access to all of our LESSONS, practice QUESTIONS, and VIDEOS.

• And, like any book, it allows you to BOOKMARK pages, UNDERLINE text, and TAKE NOTES.

• Unlike a book, however, it also allows you to design practice quizzes, create study lists, make error logs, and keep statistics on just about everything.

➢ The ┃**DESIGN a PRACTICE QUIZ**┃ feature lets you make quizzes in which you select the TOPICS, the NUMBER of questions, and the DIFFICULTY.

• It also allows you to SHUFFLE the questions by topic and difficulty and to SET a TIMER for any length of time.

• For example, you can make a 30-minute quiz comprised of fifteen intermingled Ratio, Rate, and Overlapping Sets questions, in which all the questions are advanced. Or you can make a 10-minute quiz with just ten Probability questions, of which some are easy and others are intermediate. You can pretty much make any sort of quiz that you like.

> ➤ AFTER each quiz, you get to REVIEW your performance, question by question, and to view video solutions.

• You also get to see the difficultly level of your quiz questions, as well as the time it took you to answer each of them.

• You even get to COMPARE your performance to that of other users. You see how frequently other users were able to solve the questions on your quiz and how long it took them, on average, to do so.

> ➤ As you read through our lessons, the $\boxed{\textbf{MAKE a STUDY LIST}}$ feature allows you to form a personalized study list.

• With the tap of a button, you can add any topic that you read about to an automated "to do" list, which organizes the topics you've selected by chapter and subject.

• From your study list, you can then access these topics instantly to revisit them whenever you need to.

> ➤ Similarly, the $\boxed{\textbf{CREATE an ERROR LOG}}$ feature allows you to compile a list of practice problems you wish to redo for further practice.

• Every time you answer a question, you can add it to this log, regardless of whether you got the question right or wrong, or left it blank.

• By doing so, you can keep track of every problem that you find challenging and redo them until they no longer pose a challenge.

> ➤ Finally, the app $\boxed{\textbf{TRACKS your PERFORMANCE}}$ at every turn to help you identify your strengths and weaknesses.

• In addition to the data from your practice quizzes, the app provides key information on how you're performing, by TOPIC and across DIFFICUTLY LEVELS.

• So if you want to know what percentage of advanced level Algebra questions you're answering correctly, the app can tell you. Likewise, if you want to know what percentage of intermediate level Triangle questions you're answering correctly, the app can tell you that too.

> ➤ The app offers the first volume of Master Key to the GRE for $\boxed{\textbf{FREE}}$. The other four volumes retail for $9.99 apiece.

(6) Register Your Book! – Every volume of <u>Master Key to the GRE</u> comes with six months of free access to our collection of video solutions.

- If you have a print edition of <u>Master Key</u>, you'll need to Register your book(s) to access these videos.

  ➢ To do so, please go to **www.sherpaprep.com/activate** and enter your email address, last name, and shipping address.

- **Be sure to provide the SAME last name and shipping address that you used to purchase your copy of <u>Master Key to the GRE</u>.**

- If you received your books upon enrolling in a GRE prep course with **Sherpa Prep**, be sure to enter the same last name and shipping address that you used to enroll.

  ➢ Once you've entered this information, you will be asked to create an account password.

- Please RECORD this password! You will need it to login to our website whenever you choose to watch our videos.

- Our login page can be found at **www.sherpaprep.com/videos**. We recommend that you BOOKMARK this page for future visits.

  ➢ If your registration is **Unsuccessful**, please send your last name and shipping address to **sales@sherpaprep.com**.

- We will confirm your purchase manually and create a login account for you.

- In most cases, this process will take no more than a few hours. Please note, however, that requests can take up to 24 hours to fulfill if you submit your request on a U.S. federal holiday or if we are experiencing extremely heavy demand.

  ➢ Six months after your date of registration, your video access to <u>Master Key to the GRE</u> will come to an end.

- An additional six months of access can be purchased at a rate of $9.99 per book. To do so, simply login at **www.sherpaprep.com/videos** and follow the directions.

About the GRE

(7) The Structure of the GRE – Before examining the content of the GRE, let's take a moment to discuss how the exam is structured and administered.

• The GRE is a computer-based exam that is offered world-wide on a daily basis.

> The test consists of six sections and takes around 3 hours and 45 minutes to complete (not including breaks).

• These sections are as follows:

    I.   An Analytical Writing section containing two essays.
    II. Two Verbal Reasoning sections.
    III. Two Quantitative Reasoning sections.
    IV. One Unidentified Research section.

• The Analytical Writing section is always first, while **the other five sections may appear in ANY order**. You get a 10-minute break between the third and fourth sections, and a 1-minute break between the other test sections.

> The Unidentified Research section **does NOT count towards your score** and is either a Verbal Reasoning section or a Quantitative Reasoning section.

• Unfortunately, the Unidentified Research section is designed to look exactly like the other sections — there is no way to spot it.

• As such, you must take all five sections seriously. Even though one of them will not count towards your score, there is no way of knowing which section that is.

> Finally, some exams have an **Identified Research section** in place of the Unidentified Research section.

• This section is marked "For Research Purposes" and does not count towards your score. If your exam has an Identified Research section, it will appear at the end of the test.

• On the following page, you'll find a breakdown of all six sections. Notice that every Quantitative Reasoning section has 20 questions and is 35 minutes long.

• Similarly, notice that every Verbal Reasoning section also has 20 questions but is only 30 minutes long.

> ➤ When viewing the table below, remember that **the order of sections 2 through 6 is RANDOM**. These sections can occur in any order.

• This means that the Unidentified Research section can be ANY section after the first and that you might get two Quantitative sections in a row (or two Verbal sections)!

Section	Task	Number of Questions	Time	Note
1	Analytical Writing	Two Essays	30 minutes per essay	
2	Verbal Reasoning	20	30 minutes	
3	Quantitative Reasoning	20	35 minutes	
10-minute break				
4	Verbal Reasoning	20	30 minutes	
5	Quantitative Reasoning	20	35 minutes	
6	Unidentified Research	20	30 or 35 minutes	Not scored

• Also remember that that Unidentified Research section may be replaced with an Identified Research section. If so, the Identified Research section will appear at the end of the test.

(8) The Scoring System – After your GRE has been completed and graded, you will receive three scores:

1. A Verbal Reasoning score.
2. A Quantitative Reasoning score.
3. An Analytical Writing score.

- **Both the Verbal Reasoning and Quantitative Reasoning scores are reported on a scale from 130 to 170, in one-point increments**.

  ➢ The Analytical Writing score is reported on a scale from 0 to 6, in half-point increments.

- A score of NS (no score) is given for any measure in which no questions (or essay prompts) are answered.

- In addition to these scaled scores, you will also receive percentile rankings, which compare your scores to those of other GRE test-takers.

  ➢ Before applying to graduate school or business school, you should have a basic sense of what constitutes a good score and what constitutes a bad score.

- Currently, **an average Verbal Reasoning score is 151, an average Quantitative Reasoning score is 152, and an average Analytical Writing score is approximately 3.5**.

- Roughly two-thirds of all test-takers receive a score within the following ranges:

1. Verbal Reasoning: 142 to 159
2. Quantitative Reasoning: 143 to 161
3. Analytical Writing: 3 to 4.5

  ➢ As a loose guideline, these ranges suggest that any score in the 160s is fairly exceptional and that any score in the 130s may raise a red flag with an admissions committee.

- The same goes for Analytical Writing scores higher than 4.5 or lower than 3. In fact, only 7 percent of test-takers receive a score above 4.5 and only 9 percent receive a score below 3.

- You can find a complete concordance of GRE scores and their percentile equivalents on page 23 of this document: **http://www.ets.org/s/gre/pdf/gre_guide.pdf**.

➤ As you prepare for the GRE, we strongly encourage you to research the programs to which you plan to apply.

• Get a general sense of what sorts of scores your programs are looking for. See whether they have "cutoff" scores below which they no longer consider applicants.

• Knowing what you need to achieve is important. If your program needs an elite math score, it's best to know immediately so that you can make time to prepare properly!

➤ In some cases, you'll find the information you need online. In many cases, however, you'll need to contact your program directly.

• If you are reluctant to do so, bear this in mind: many programs are more forthcoming about scores in person or over the phone than they are by email or on the internet.

• Moreover, it never hurts to make contact with a prospective program. Saying "hi" gives you a chance to ask important questions and — if you can present yourself intelligently and professionally — to make a good impression on a potential committee member.

➤ If a school tells you they are looking for applicants with an average score of 160 per section, remember that such quotes are only averages!

• Some applicants will be accepted with scores below those averages and some will be turned down with scores above them.

• An average is simply a "ballpark" figure that you want to shoot for. Coming up short doesn't guarantee rejection (particularly if the rest of your application is strong), and achieving it doesn't ensure admission.

➤ Unfortunately, not all programs are willing to divulge average or "cutoff" GRE scores to the public.

• If that's the case with a program you're interested, here are some general pointers to keep in mind:

1. Engineering, Economics, and Hard Sciences programs are likely to place far more emphasis on your Quantitative Reasoning score than your other scores.

2. The more prestigious a university it is, the more likely its programs will demand higher scores than comparable programs at other schools.

3. Public Health, Public Policy, and International Affairs programs likely require very strong scores for all three portions of the GRE.

4. Education, Sociology, and Nursing programs are less likely to require outstanding scores.

   ➤ Should you wish to get a sense of average GRE scores, by intended field of study, you can do so here: **http://www.ets.org/s/gre/pdf/gre_guide_table4.pdf**.

• When viewing these scores, remember that these are the scores of INTENDED applicants!

• The average score of ACCEPTED applicants is likely to be higher for many programs — in some cases, much higher.

   ➤ Finally, it's worth noting that many programs use GRE scores to determine which applicants will receive SCHOLARSHIPS.

• When contacting programs, be sure to ask them about the averages or "cutoffs" for scholarship recipients.

• And if you find it difficult to study for an exam that has little to do with your intended field of study, just remember: strong GRE scores = $$$!

(9) Registering for the GRE – The GRE is administered via computer in over 160 countries on a near daily basis.

- This means that you can that you take the GRE almost ANY day of the year.

  ➢ To register, you must create a personalized GRE account, which you can do online at **http://www.ets.org/gre/revised_general/register/**.

- When creating your account, the NAME you use must MATCH the name you use to register for the GRE.

- **It must also match the name on your official identification EXACTLY**! If it doesn't, you may be prohibited from taking the exam (without refund).

  ➢ We encourage you to schedule a date that gives you ample time to prepare properly. Don't choose a random date just to get it over with!

- If possible, wait until you score a few points higher than your target score at least TWO TIMES in a row on practice exams. Doing so will ensure that you're ready to take the exam.

- When scheduling the time of day, **don't schedule an 8 a.m. exam if you are not accustomed to waking up at 6:30 a.m. or earlier**. The exam is challenging enough. Don't take it when you're likely to be groggy or weary!

  ➢ If you plan to take the exam on a specific date, register at least one month in advance. Exam centers have limited capacity, so dates can fill up quickly, especially in the fall.

- On the day of the test, be sure to bring your official identification and your GRE admission ticket.

- Once you register for the exam, your admission ticket can be printed out at any time through your personalized GRE account online.

  ➢ Finally, if you need to reschedule or cancel your exam date, you must do so no later than FOUR days before your test date. (Ten days for individuals in mainland China.)

- This means that a Saturday test date must be canceled by Tuesday and that an April 18th test date must be canceled by April 14th.

- You can find more information on canceling or rescheduling a test date here: **http://www.ets.org/gre/revised_general/register/change**.

(10) Reporting & Canceling Scores – Immediately upon completing your exam, you will be given the opportunity to cancel your scores or to report them.

• If you choose to cancel your scores, they will be deleted irreversibly.

➤ Neither you nor the programs to which you're applying will see the numbers. Your official score report, however, will indicate a canceled test.

• In general, there's almost no reason to cancel your scores.

• **The GRE has a Score Select option that allows you to decide which scores to send if you've taken the GRE more than once**. Thus, if you take the exam a second time (or a third time), you can simply choose which set of scores to report.

➤ If you choose to report your scores, you will immediately see your unofficial Quantitative Reasoning and Verbal Reasoning scores.

• Roughly 10 to 15 days after your test date, you will receive an email notifying you that your official scores and your Analytical Writing score are available.

• To view them, simply go to the personalized GRE account you created to register for the exam.

➤ You won't need to memorize any school CODES to send your scores while at the test center.

• Such codes will be accessible by computer, should you wish to report your scores when you're there. To get the code for a particular program, you'll need:

1. The name of the college (e.g. College of Arts & Sciences).
2. The name of the university.
3. The city and state of its location.

• As long as you have this information for each of your programs, you'll have everything you need to send out your score reports on the spot.

➤ **Your OFFICIAL and UNOFFICIAL scores are unlikely to differ**. If they do, the difference will almost surely be a single point.

• For example, your Verbal Reasoning score may rise from a 157 to a 158 or your Quantitative Reasoning score may dip from a 162 to a 161.

• The scores you receive on test day are an estimate comparing your performance with previous data. The official scores compare your performance with those of everyone who took that particular exam – hence the potential discrepancy.

> **Your official scores will be valid for FIVE years**. For example, a test taken on August 2nd, 2015 will be valid until August 1st, 2020.

• Over the course of those five years, your scaled scores will never change. The percentiles, however, may shift marginally.

• Thus, a scaled Verbal Reasoning score of 162 may equate to the 89th percentile in 2015. Come 2018, however, that 162 may equate to a 91st percentile.

> On test day, after viewing your unofficial scores, you will be given a choice at the test center.

• You can choose NOT to send your scores at that time or to send **free score reports** to as many as FOUR graduate programs or fellowship sponsors.

• If you choose to send out score reports at the test center, you will be given two further options:

1. The **Most Recent** option – send your scores from the test you've just completed.
2. The **All** option – send the scores from all the GREs you've taken in the last five years.

> After your test date, you can send additional score reports for a fee. **For each report**, you will be given the options above.

• **You will also be given the option to send your scores from just one exam OR from ANY exams you've taken over the last five years.**

• You cannot, however, choose your best Quantitative Reasoning score from one exam and your best Verbal Reasoning score from another. When sending scores, you must send all the scores you receive on a particular exam date.

> ➤ Given all of these options, **here's our advice**. First, NEVER cancel your scores. There's no point.

• Even if you believe you've had a bad performance, you may as well learn how you did. You never know — you might even be pleasantly surprised.

• If your scores are great, you're done. Send out your scores on test day to take advantage of the four free score reports.

> ➤ If you feel you can do better, retake the exam as soon as possible. Don't let your hard work go to waste.

• Anyone can have a bad day, misplay their time, or make an uncharacteristic number of careless errors.

• **You can retake the exam every 21 days** and up to 5 times within any 12-month period, so you won't have to wait long.

> ➤ Upon receiving your second set of scores, use the Score Select option on test day to determine which set of scores to send for free (or to send both sets).

• In the unpleasant event that you take the exam more than twice, consider utilizing the Score Select option the day after your last exam.

• This will allow you to send the single set of scores (or pair of scores) that puts you in the best possible light. Of course, if that last score is awesome, use the four free score reports to send out your most recent scores while you're at the test center!

Navigating the Exam

(11) How the Exam Works – Although the GRE is administered on computer, the exam has been designed to mimic the experience of a traditional, paper-based standardized test.

- This means that you can:

  - ☑ Skip questions and return to them later.
  - ☑ Leave questions blank.
  - ☑ Change or edit an answer.

- You can even "flag" questions with a check mark as a reminder to revisit them before time expires. (As with a paper-based exam, however, you cannot return to a section once that section ends.)

  - ➢ If you took the GRE before 2011, you'll notice that this format differs dramatically from the one you remember.

- **The exam is no longer adaptive on a question-by-question basis**, so the problems don't get harder if you answer a prior problem correctly.

- In fact, you can now preview every question within a section the moment that section begins. (If you like, you can even do the problems in reverse order.)

  - ➢ There are, however, a few differences between the way the GRE works and that of most paper-based standardized tests.

- First, the questions in each section do NOT get progressively harder.

- Unlike, say, the SAT, where the first questions within a section are generally easy and the last questions within a section are generally hard, **the difficulty of GRE questions varies throughout a particular section**. In other words, a section might start with a hard question and end with an easy question.

  - ➢ Furthermore, the GRE has a "Review Screen" that allows you to see which questions you've answered and which ones you haven't.

- The Review Screen can also be used to see which questions you've flagged for further review. (A very helpful feature!)

> ➤ **Finally, the GRE adapts on a section-by-section basis.** If you perform well on your first quantitative section, your second quantitative section will be harder.

• Likewise, if you do not perform well on your first quantitative section, your second quantitative section will be easier.

• The verbal sections work this way, too. The quantitative and verbal sections, however, are independent of one another. A strong performance on a verbal section will not result in more difficult quantitative sections, or vice versa.

> ➤ According to our experiments with the GRE's official test software, **how you perform on your first quantitative section can produce 1 of 3 results.**

• The same is true of your performance on the first verbal section:

Approximate # of Correct Questions on First Section	Difficulty Level of Second Section
0 to 6	Easy
7 to 13	Medium
14 to 20	Hard

• In some exams, it might take 15 correct answers to end up with a hard second section. In others, it might take 13. The correlation between the number of questions you get right and the difficulty level of your second section, however, generally matches the chart above.

> ➤ Our experiments also indicate that **the difficulty of the questions that you get right has no bearing on the difficulty level of the second section**.

• In other words, getting any 14 (or so) questions correct will give you a hard second section — it doesn't matter whether those questions are the hardest 14 or the easiest 14.

• It also doesn't matter how quickly you answer anything. There are no bonus points for solving problems quickly.

> ➤ It should, however, be noted that **a hard second section is not comprised entirely of hard questions**, nor an easy second section entirely of easy questions.

• The questions in ANY section span a range of difficulties. A hard second section simply has a greater number of hard questions than an easy one. Thus, if you receive easy questions in your second quantitative section, it does not mean that you've done poorly!

(12) The Scoring Algorithm – Exactly how the GRE is scored is a closely guarded secret.

• From the official practice test software, however, it's clear that Quantitative Reasoning and Verbal Reasoning scores are essentially the byproducts of two factors:

1. How many questions you answer correctly.
2. Whether your second sections are easy, medium, or hard.

• As you may recall from our discussion of the structure of the GRE, every exam has two Quantitative Reasoning sections and two Verbal Reasoning sections that count.

➤ Since each of these sections has 20 questions, every GRE has 40 Quantitative Reasoning questions and 40 Verbal Reasoning questions.

• As you may also recall, each of these measures is scored on a 41-point scale (from 130 to 170). This means, that **each question is essentially worth 1 point**.

• Thus, to get a Quantitative Reasoning score of 170, you likely need to answer all 40 questions correctly. Each question that you get wrong more or less subtracts 1 point from your score.

➤ In analyzing the practice test software, however, it's also apparent that there are deductions for failing to achieve a hard or medium second section.

• In general, these deductions range from 1 to 3 points.

• For example, if you were to get 11 questions correct on your first Quantitative Reasoning section, your score would be lowered 9 points on account of the 9 questions you got wrong or left blank since the exam treats blank and incorrect answers equally. (**There is NO PENALTY for getting problems wrong, so always GUESS when you're stuck!**)

➤ Your 11 correct answers, however, would also result in a second section of medium difficulty.

• Thus, your score would be lowered an additional 1 to 3 points for failing to make it to the hard section.

• Likewise, if you were to answer only 4 questions correctly in your first Quantitative Reasoning section, your score would be lowered 16 points for the blank or incorrect answers, 1 to 3 points for failing to make it to the hard section, and another 1 to 3 points for failing to make it to the medium section.

> ➤ Thus, a test taker who gets 10 questions right in each of his or her Quantitative Reasoning sections would likely receive a score from 147 to 149.

• The 20 questions left blank or answered incorrectly would deduct 20 points from the total score.

• Failing to make it to the hard section would deduct an additional 1 to 3 points. Subtracted from 170 (a perfect score), this would leave a final score of 147 to 149:

170	A perfect score
10	10 missed questions in section 1
10	10 missed questions in section 2
− 1 to 3	The penalty for not reaching the hard section
147 to 149	

> ➤ In all likelihood, the scoring algorithm considers a few other factors as well.

• For example, when exam-makers opt to include a greater number of difficult questions on a particular exam, they likely slide the scale for that exam 1 to 2 points in order to normalize its data with past exams that contain fewer difficult questions.

• From what we've seen, however, the dynamics described above will predict your score perfectly in most instances.

(13) Strategy & Time Management – Given the factors we've just discussed, there are several tactics that we recommend when taking the GRE.

1. SKIP around.

• It doesn't matter which questions you get right, so you may as well work on the questions that are easiest for you first.

> **Don't waste your time on a question that you don't understand or that confuses you.**

• Engaging such questions will only take time from questions that may be easier for you. If you come across something that makes you nauseous, FLAG IT and double back after you've solved the questions that you know how to solve.

2. FOCUS on your FAVORITE 15.

• As we've seen, there are potentially harsh deductions for failing to achieve a hard or medium second section.

> Since reaching the hard second section generally demands a minimum of 13 to 15 correct responses, we encourage you to focus your efforts on the 15 easiest questions.

• You shouldn't ignore the hardest 5 questions, but you should save them for last. **If you don't think you can answer 15 questions correctly, focus your efforts on the easiest 10 questions.** Landing in the lowest tier can devastate your score.

3. GUESS on questions that you don't understand.

• We've also seen that an incorrect answer is no worse than a blank answer, so you may as well guess on anything that you don't understand and flag it for further review. Remember, there's no penalty for guessing!

> As you'll see, **there's either a 1 in 5 chance or a 1 in 4 chance of guessing most GRE questions correctly.**

• Those chances increase if you can eliminate a couple of answer choices through logic. If you have time left over, you can return to the questions you've flagged after you've answered everything else.

4. REMEMBER the "Two-and-a-Half Minute Rule" .

• Over the years at Sherpa Prep, we've noticed that test-takers who take more than 2.5 minutes to solve a question do so correctly only 25% of the time.

> Given that there are usually five answers to choose from, the odds of guessing correctly are 20%. If you can eliminate bad answer choices, those odds rise further!

• We know that it's tempting to battle questions to the end, especially if you "think" you can solve them. **Stubbornly hanging on, however, is a sure way to MANGLE your score**.

• Doing so wastes time (time that could be used to solve other problems) and is no more likely to result in a correct answer than guessing.

> So, if you find yourself stuck on a particular question, do yourself a favor: flag the question, then guess.

• If you can eliminate answer choices before doing so, great. Obeying the "2.5 minute rule" will help you save time for the questions at the end of the exam and avoid the debilitating panic that comes upon realizing that you've squandered your time.

5. Don't work TOO QUICKLY.

• We know that time is a critical factor on the GRE and that the exam-makers don't give you much of it.

> **Working at a frenzied pace, however, will only result in one thing — careless errors. A lot of them.**

• The key to saving time is obeying the "2.5 minute rule" and learning the right way to solve each type of problem – not working at breakneck speeds.

• If you know how to solve a problem, take the time to do so properly. You may not have time to triple check your work, but you do have time to work through any problem with care.

> **Watch out, however, for any question that you can solve in 10 seconds or fewer**.

• While there are plenty of GRE problems that can be solved in 10 seconds, exam-makers often design questions to take advantage of quick assumptions. Taking an extra 10 seconds to ensure that you haven't missed something is a great way to catch potential traps!

(14) Practice Tests – As you work through <u>Master Key to the GRE</u>, we strongly encourage you to take a practice exam every week or two.

• Success on the GRE is not just the byproduct of mastering its content — it also demands good test-taking skills.

> ➤ **Taking practice exams will help you build stamina and improve your time management.**

• Remember, the GRE takes nearly four hours to complete. Learning how to deal with the fatigue you'll encounter is part of the battle!

• The same is true of the pacing of the exam. If you don't master the speed at which you need to work, you can easily sabotage your score by working too quickly or too leisurely.

> ➤ Before you take the GRE, we encourage you to **take a minimum of SIX practice exams**.

• If you're like most test-takers, you'll need anywhere from six to eight practice exams to properly familiarize yourself with the GRE.

• For the first few — don't bother with the essays. As you begin your preparation, your time is better spent studying new material and reviewing what you've learned. Towards the end of your preparation, however, your practice exams should be full-blown dress rehearsals.

> ➤ **There are a number of different practice exams available online. Of these, only two are produced by the ETS, the company that designs the GRE.**

• At no cost, you can download the software that runs these exams from the following address: **http://www.ets.org/gre/revised_general/prepare/powerprep2/**.

• These exams have been designed to work on both Macs and PCs. As long as your computer's operating system and software are reasonably up to date, you should be able to use them on any computer.

> ➤ For additional exams, almost any of the available options will do. While they all have issues of one sort or another, most are reasonable facsimiles of the GRE.

• When taking such exams, however, please bear in mind that they are NOT the real thing. Some of their questions are unrealistic and their score predictions, though roughly accurate, are best taken with a grain of salt.

> ➤ Whenever you take a practice exam, it's important that you **make the experience as REALISTIC as possible**.

• Doing things you can't do on test day will only corrupt your practice results and prevent you from adopting helpful habits.

• If you can, take each exam in one sitting and resist the urge to pause the test or to use outside help. Likewise, refrain from drinking or eating during your tests. No coffee, no water, no snacks. Save these things for your 10-minute break between sections 3 and 4.

> ➤ Remember, you're preparing for a stressful "brain marathon" that's essentially 4-hours long. You'll need STAMINA to be successful.

• Figure out how much you need to eat and drink before your test. Figure out what to eat during your break. Identify the kind of foods that suit you best.

• The same goes for your bathroom habits. At the exam center, you can't pause the test to go to the bathroom. So, use your practice exams to learn how your eating habits affect your bodily needs! "Holding it in" for over an hour is a brutal way to take this test.

> ➤ As you take your practice exams, do your best to **stay off the "emotional rollercoaster"**. Don't get too high when things go well.

• And don't get too down if your scores don't shoot up instantly. Improving GRE scores is hard work.

• For some people, progress is a slow, steady crawl. For others, it's an uneven process, filled with periods of stagnation, occasional drops, and dramatic increases.

> ➤ However your exams may be going, keep grinding away! Stay focused on your goals and keep up the hard work.

• Test-takers who prepare like professionals — who keep an even keel, who do their assignments properly, and who commit to improving their weaknesses — ALWAYS achieve their goals in the end.

• As we tell our students, preparing for the GRE is like going to the gym. It may take you a while to get in shape, but ANYONE can do so if they put in the time and train properly.

➤ **After you complete each practice exam, go through it carefully and learn from your mistakes.**

• See whether you can identify any trends in your performance. Are you working too quickly and making careless errors? Are you struggling with the same topics repeatedly?

• Are you running out of time because you're violating the "2.5 minute rule"? Do you start off strong and then taper off as the test goes along? Does it take you half an hour to get "locked in" and then get better as you go?

➤ A lot of people believe they are "bad test-takers". This is nonsense. The reality is that people get questions wrong for tangible reasons.

• Analyzing your mistakes when the "game is real" will allow you to PINPOINT those reasons so you can ADDRESS them.

• To help you become a more "self-aware" test-taker, we encourage you to fill out the following table every time you complete an exam:

	Knew How to Solve	Didn't Know How to Solve
Correct	Bravo!	Luck
Incorrect	Carelessness?	**Expected**

➤ If you get a question wrong because you don't know how to solve it, see whether you can identify its TOPIC or notice any TRENDS.

• For example, you might notice that a lot of your mistakes involve Algebra. If so, that's a clear indication that you need to improve your Algebra skills.

• If you get a question wrong despite knowing how to solve it, see whether you can figure out how it happened. Did you misread the question? Did you write down information incorrectly? Did you make a silly math error?

➤ Mistakes such as these are often the result of RUSHING, which in turn is generally the byproduct of poor time management elsewhere.

• So keep track, to the best of your abilities, of whether you are finishing your sections too quickly or are making frantic efforts to finish because you're violating the "2.5 minute rule" too frequently. Both scenarios generally lead to a host of careless mistakes that will sabotage your progress.

Intro to Quantitative Reasoning

(15) Content Overview – The quantitative portion of the GRE is designed to measure your ability to think <u>smartly</u> about math — to find simple solutions to problems that seem complicated.

• The problems that you'll encounter may appear difficult or time-consuming, but there's ALWAYS a straightforward way to solve them.

> ➤ In terms of content, the GRE solely tests concepts that you learned in high school or use in everyday life.

• These concepts fall into four categories:

> 1. Arithmetic, Algebra, and Number Properties
> 2. Word Problems
> 3. Data Interpretation
> 4. Geometry

> ➤ You won't find any Calculus or Trigonometry on the GRE, nor will you find some of the more sophisticated forms of Algebra typically taught in an Algebra II course.

• That's because the emphasis of this exam is on your ability to reason.

• By limiting the content to the topics listed above, the GRE becomes less about "what you know" (everyone studied those topics in high school) and more about your ability to APPLY commonly known information and to think logically.

> ➤ This said, don't be fooled into thinking that GRE math can't be sophisticated. The exam demands that you know these topics EXTREMELY well.

• To be successful on the GRE, you'll need to relearn everything you learned about them (or were supposed to learn) back in high school.

• And, if you want to solve the most advanced questions, you'll need to learn a few intricacies that you almost surely were never taught.

➤ Based on our analysis of the official exam materials released to the public, roughly one-third of GRE questions focus on Arithmetic, Algebra, and Number Properties.

• Approximately 33% are Word Problems and a little more than a third involve Geometry or the interpretation of Charts and Graphs:

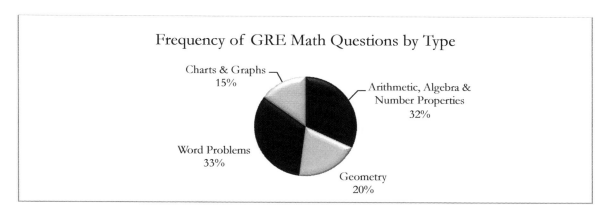

Frequency of GRE Math Questions by Type

Charts & Graphs 15%
Arithmetic, Algebra & Number Properties 32%
Word Problems 33%
Geometry 20%

• When viewing the diagram above, bear in mind that Word Problems and problems involving Geometry or Charts and Graphs often demand the use of Algebra and Arithmetic. Thus, in many ways, Algebra and Arithmetic are even more critical to your success than the diagram above suggests.

➤ Volume 1 of <u>Master Key to the GRE</u> is devoted to **Arithmetic & "Plan B" Strategies**.

• Here, you'll find discussion of such topics as:

Arithmetic Shortcuts	Strategies for "Smart Math"
Essential Number Lists	Strategies for Using the Answer Choices
Fractions	Number Picking Strategies
Decimals	Strategies for Guessing
Digit Problems	

➤ Volume 2 is dedicated to **Number Properties & Algebra**. Among the topics you'll find covered are:

Factors & Multiples	Exponents & Roots
Prime Factorization	The Properties of Evens & Odds
Number Line Problems	Algebra
Absolute Value	Functions, Sequences & Symbolism
Remainder Problems	

> ➤ Our discussion of **Word Problems** is divided between Volumes 3 and 4. Volume 3 focuses on topics such as:

Percents	Algebraic Word Problems
Mixtures	Age Problems
Alterations	Overlapping Sets
Ratios & Proportions	Exponential & Linear Growth
Rate Problems	

• Volume 4 examines **Statistics & Data Interpretation**.

> ➤ Among the various chapters of Volume 4, you'll find discussions of a wide range of topics, including:

Means, Medians & Modes	Probability
Weighed Averages	Combinatorics
Standard Deviation	Bar Graphs & Line Graphs
Quartiles & Boxplots	Pie Charts & Data Tables
Normal Distributions	Multi-Figure Data Sets
Equally Spaced Number Sets	

• Finally, Volume 5 is devoted to **Geometry**.

> ➤ Here, you'll find a detailed treatment of everything you may have been taught in high-school but have probably forgotten.

• The major topics include:

Lines & Angles	Rectangular Solids
Triangles	Cylinders
Quadrilaterals	Coordinate Geometry
Polygons	
Circles	

• If all of this seems intimidating, don't worry! We promise you: <u>Master Key to the GRE</u> will show you just how simple these concepts can be.

(16) Problem Solving Questions – Before we get started, let's take a few pages to discuss the ways in which the GRE formats its math questions.

• As you may recall, every GRE has two Quantitative Reasoning sections. Since each of these sections has 20 questions, your exam will feature a total of 40 math questions (that actually count).

> ➤ 25 of these will be "Problem Solving" questions and 15 will be "Quantitative Comparison" questions.

• If you've taken standardized tests before, Problem Solving questions will be familiar to you. Here's an example:

If $x + y > 14$ and $x = 2y + 8$, then which of the following must be true?

(A) $y < -3$ (B) $y < -2$ (C) $y = 0$ (D) $y > 2$ (E) $y > 4$

Answer: D. To answer questions in this format, you simply need to select the answer choice that represents the correct answer.

> ➤ Here, for example, we've been told that $x = 2y + 8$. Thus, we can rewrite $x + y > 14$ as follows, by substituting $2y + 8$ for x:

Replace x with $2y + 8$

$\longrightarrow (2y + 8) + y > 14$

• To simplify the Algebra, we can drop the parentheses and subtract 8 from both sides of the inequality. Doing so proves that the correct is (D), since:

$2y + 8 + y > 14$	Drop the parentheses.
$2y + y > 6$	Subtract 8 from both sides.
$3y > 6$	Add $2y + y$.
$y > 2$	Divide both sides by 3.

• If the math doesn't make sense here, don't worry! This question is simply intended to show you what a Problem Solving question looks like. The math behind it is covered in our book on Number Properties & Algebra.

(17) "Select One or More" Questions – From time to time, Problem Solving questions will prompt you to select one or more answer choices.

• On a typical exam, each quantitative section will contain (at most) one or two of these questions.

   ➤ "Select One or More" questions are easy to spot — they always ask you to "indicate <u>all</u> such values".

• What's more, **the answer choices are always in square boxes**. In regular Problem Solving questions, the answer choices are circled.

• According to the Official Guide to the GRE revised General Test, the directions for such questions are always as follows:

    <u>**Directions:**</u> **Select ONE or MORE answer choices according to the specific directions.**

• If the question does not specify how many answer choices to select, you must select ALL that apply. The correct answer may be just one of the choices or as many as all of the choices. **There must, however, be at least one correct answer.**

   ➤ The exam-makers further specify that no credit is given unless you select all of the correct answers and no others. In other words, there is NO PARTIAL credit.

• Thus, if there are two correct answers, and you only select one, the GRE gives you zero credit. The same is true if there are three correct answers and you select four.

• Let's take a look at a sample question:

If $-2 \leq x \leq 8$ and $-4 \leq y \leq 3$, which of the following could represent the value of xy?

Indicate <u>all</u> such values.

   $\boxed{\text{A}}$ −40 $\boxed{\text{B}}$ −32 $\boxed{\text{C}}$ 7 $\boxed{\text{D}}$ 15 $\boxed{\text{E}}$ 32

Answer: B, C, and D. Notice that there are two clues indicating that we may need to select more than one answer here.

- First, the question asks us to "indicate all such values". **Additionally, the answer choices are in boxes.**

  ➤ To answer this question, we first need to determine the range of possible values for xy.

- We can do so by identifying the greatest and smallest possible values for x and y.

- According to the problem, $-2 \leq x \leq 8$ and $-4 \leq y \leq 3$. Thus, the greatest and smallest values for each variable are:

$$x = -2 \text{ and } 8 \qquad\qquad y = -4 \text{ and } 3$$

  ➤ Next, we can **test all four combinations** of x times y to determine the largest and smallest values of xy.

- If x can be as small as -2 and as large as 8, and y can be as small as -3 and as large as 4, then those combinations would be:

Combo #1	Combo #2	Combo #3	Combo #4
$(-2)(-4) = 8$	$(-2)(3) = -6$	$(8)(-4) = -32$	$(8)(3) = 24$

  ➤ As we can see from these combinations, the greatest possible value of x times y is 24 and the smallest possible value is -32.

- Thus, the range of values for xy extends from -32 to 24. Algebraically, this can be stated as $-32 \leq xy \leq 24$.

- Since -32, 7, and 15 all fall within the range of value from -32 to 24, **we must select $\boxed{B}$, $\boxed{C}$, and $\boxed{D}$, and nothing more, to get credit for this question.** If we fail to select all three answer choices, or select a fourth, our response would be considered incorrect.

  ➤ Again, if the math doesn't make sense here, don't worry! This question is simply intended to show you what a "Select One or More" question looks like.

- The math behind it is covered in our book on Number Properties & Algebra.

Chapter 1: Introduction

(18) Numeric Entry Questions – On each of your quantitative sections, anywhere from one to three of your Problem Solving questions will ask you for a "Numeric Entry".

• Numeric Entry questions prompt you to **type a numeric answer into a box** below the problem.

➢ Such questions tend to be more difficult than other Problem Solving questions since you can't use the answer choices to determine whether you're on the right track.

• Further, it's almost impossible to guess the correct answer. With regular Problem Solving questions, you at least have a 1 in 5 chance of getting lucky.

• Let's take a look at a sample question:

When walking, a person takes 24 complete steps in 15 seconds. At this rate, how many steps does this person take in 5 seconds?

• There are several ways to solve a problem like this. Perhaps the easiest way is to set up a proportion:

$$\frac{24 \text{ steps}}{15 \text{ seconds}} = \frac{x \text{ steps}}{5 \text{ seconds}}$$

• When comparing the bottoms of the two fractions, notice that "15 seconds" is exactly three times as large as "5 seconds".

➢ With proportions, the relationship between the tops of the fractions is the same as that between the bottoms.

• In other words, "24 steps" must be three times as large as "x steps", since "15 seconds" is three times as large as "5 seconds".

• Thus, $x = 8$, because 24 is three times as large as 8. To solve this problem, therefore, **we would need to type 8 into the numeric entry box** beneath the question.

➢ As with the previous sections, don't worry if the math doesn't make sense here! This question is simply intended to show you what a Numeric Entry question looks like.

• The math behind it is covered properly in our book on Word Problems.

(19) Quantitative Comparisons – The rest of your math questions will prompt you to compare two quantities.

• Such questions, commonly known as "Quantitative Comparisons", consist of two quantities, labeled Quantity A and Quantity B, and, in many cases, some additional information.

  ➤ Beneath the two quantities you'll find four answer choices, asking which of the two quantities is LARGER. The answer choices are always the SAME.

• **MEMORIZE them IMMEDIATELY.** 15 of your 40 math questions will be in this format. If you spend 10 seconds wading through the answer choices on each of these questions, you'll be wasting 2.5 minutes of your exam!

• Let's take a look at a sample problem:

$$xy \geq 1$$

Quantity A	**Quantity B**
xy	$(xy)^3$

    (A) **Quantity A is greater.**
    (B) **Quantity B is greater.**
    (C) **The quantities are equal.**
    (D) **The relationship cannot be determined**
             from the information given.

Answer. D. At the top of the problem, we are told that $xy \geq 1$. This means that xy can be any value equal to or greater than one.

  ➤ If $xy = 1$, notice that the quantities are equal, since $(1)^3 = 1 \times 1 \times 1 = 1$. If $xy = 2$, however, notice that Quantity B is greater than Quantity A, since $(2)^3 = 2 \times 2 \times 2 = 8$.

• Because the two quantities can be equal or can be different, we cannot determine which quantity is larger from the given information. The correct answer is therefore (D).

• Any time two quantities have an INCONSISTENT RELATIONSHIP — i.e. any time that A can be greater than or equal to B or that B can be greater than or equal to A — the relationship between the two quantities CANNOT be determined.

(20) Before You Get Started – If you've read through the preceding pages, you're ready to get started.

• Before you do, we'd like to offer you a last few bits of advice. We know that many people who take the GRE are not very comfortable with math.

➤ If you're one of them, you may have been told at an early age that you weren't a "math person" or that your brain "doesn't work that way".

• That's total nonsense. The truth is that EVERYONE can learn the sort of math required by the GRE.

• Yes, it may require hard work — especially if you haven't done math in over a decade. But you CAN do it. Don't let the idiotic assessment of a bad teacher or a misogynist prevent you from attaining your goals.

➤ As you begin to practice, **DON'T try to do everything in your head**. Scratch work is an IMPORTANT part of the problem solving process.

• Taking notes will SPEED you up and help you avoid careless errors.

• Make sure, however, that your writing is organized and legible. Sloppy handwriting is a sure path to careless errors. Writing the work for one problem atop the work for another problem is even worse. (Yes, some people do this.)

➤ Likewise, **make sure that your handwriting is appropriately sized**. If you can solve twenty problems on a single sheet of paper, your writing is too small.

• Yes, the GRE only provides you with a few sheets of unlined scratch paper, but you can always raise your hand to trade for new sheets BEFORE you run out.

• Conversely, if you're using one sheet of paper per question, write smaller. You shouldn't need to request paper frequently. Divide your sheets of scratch paper into six equal sections. With proper penmanship, you should be able to fit the work for any problem in one of the sections.

➤ When solving problems, **beware of crazy decimals or fractions**. If your scratch work involves something like $0.123 \times \frac{7}{13}$, you're doing something wrong.

• In general, the GRE tends to use "smart numbers" — numbers that are designed to yield simple results under the proper analysis.

- When the GRE uses exotic numbers, the exam is almost always testing your ability to identify patterns or relationships (e.g. $0.\overline{54} = \frac{5}{9}$) or to approximate.

  ➤ If you're worried about anxiety, preparing THOROUGHLY for the GRE is the best way to beat test-taking jitters.

- Nothing calms unsteady nerves more than seeing problems you KNOW how to solve because the content is EASY for you.

- You should also **set up a test date that allows you enough time to schedule a retake**, if necessary. (Remember, you can take the GRE every 21 days and up to 5 times a year.) Knowing that you'll have a second shot at the GRE can take the pressure off your first exam.

  ➤ On test day, bring food and water with you to the exam center. You'll be there for nearly five hours.

- Doing anything for that length of time is fatiguing. Eating a few nuts and a piece of fruit before your exam (and during your break) will help keep you sharp.

- Just be sure to steer clear of drinking too much water or consuming too much sugar or caffeine. You don't want to take multiple bathroom breaks while your exam is running or to crash during the final hour of your test.

  ➤ If you can, **get to the test center early**. Taking the GRE is stressful enough. You don't want to exacerbate that stress by running late.

- Plan to get there a half hour in advance. If you're commuting to an unfamiliar area, research the commute carefully and allot an additional 15 minutes (in case you get lost).

- Once inside (don't forget your ID and admissions ticket!), use the extra time to warm up with a few practice problems or to review your notes. Doing so will help get your brain "in gear" before your exam.

  ➤ Finally, **brace yourself for broken air-conditioners, sniffling neighbors, and unfriendly staffers**.

- Although test centers are generally well run, it's important to remember that there can be problems.

- As long as you dress in layers, however, and make use of the headphones or earplugs that are supplied with your exam, these issues shouldn't pose you any problems.

Arithmetic

Arithmetic

To be discussed:

Fundamental Concepts

Whether you're aiming for a perfect score or a score closer to average, mastery of the following lists and concepts will help you work with numbers more quickly and easily.

1   Introduction
2   PEMDAS: the Order of Operations
3   The Calculator
4   Time: the Hidden Topic
5   Know Your Multiplication Tables
6   Squares, Cubes, and Special Powers
7   Square Roots From 1 to 10
8   Fraction to Decimal Equivalents: the "Conversion List"

Arithmetic Shortcuts

Like the lists and concepts above, the following shortcuts will improve the speed of your calculations. That speed will save you valuable minutes over the course of your exam.

9   The "Multiplication Trick"
10   Chunking: the Division Shortcut
11   Number Tricks
12   The Addition Shortcut
13   Subtraction by Addition

14   Quick Percents
15   The Divisibility Rules

Practice Questions

There's no substitute for elbow grease. Practice your new skills to ensure that you internalize what you've studied.

16   Problem Sets
17   Solutions

Fundamental Concepts

(1) Introduction – Of all the concepts tested by the revised GRE, none are more important than those of Arithmetic, Number Properties, and Algebra.

• Not only do a third of GRE questions test these concepts directly, but **a majority of the other questions also involve these concepts**.

> ➤ Word problems, Geometry problems, and problems involving Charts and Graphs all demand the ability to work easily with numbers and to solve for *x*.

• In other words, these concepts are the "heart" of GRE math: we can't solve the exotic concepts without them!

• Of the problems that test Arithmetic, Number Properties, and Algebra directly, roughly 35% focus on Algebra; 25% focus on Integer Properties; 20% focus on Exponents and Roots; 12.5% focus on Fractions or Decimals; and 7.5% focus on Functions.

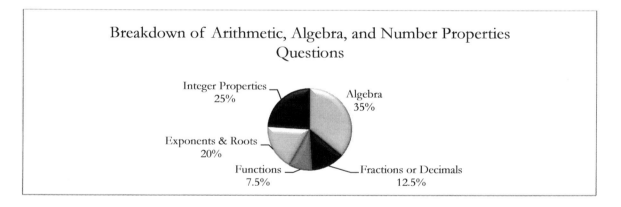

Breakdown of Arithmetic, Algebra, and Number Properties Questions

Integer Properties 25%
Algebra 35%
Exponents & Roots 20%
Functions 7.5%
Fractions or Decimals 12.5%

• You may notice that our pie chart does not contain a section specifically labeled "Arithmetic" or "Simple Math Skills". The reason for this is simple: very few GRE questions solely test your basic math skills.

> ➤ From this, you might mistakenly assume that strong arithmetic skills are not important for the GRE. Don't be fooled! They're vital.

• Although few questions solely test your arithmetic skills, almost all questions require the ability to work with numbers quickly.

(2) PEMDAS: the Order of Operations – Whenever you perform arithmetic, there is a specific order in which the arithmetic must be performed.

- This order is commonly known through the acronym PEMDAS, which stands for:

P = Parentheses
E = Exponents
M = Multiplication
D = Division
A = Addition
S = Subtraction

> PEMDAS represents the **universally agreed upon** order of arithmetic operations. To get a sense of how the order of operations works, consider the following:

Quantity A	**Quantity B**
$1 + 4(5 - 3)^2 - 3 \times 6$	-1

Answer: C. Although we may be tempted to solve this problem by working from left to right, **doing so would be incorrect.**

- To solve this problem correctly, we have to follow the ordering of PEMDAS.

> To start, we must first resolve the problem's **parentheses** and then its **exponent**. We can do this by resolving $5 - 3$ and squaring the result:

$$1 + 4(2)^2 - 3 \times 6 \rightarrow 1 + 4(4) - 3 \times 6$$

- Next, we must resolve the problem's multiplication. Notice that there are two instances of multiplication: 4(4) and 3×6.

- **If your problem contains two or more instances of the same operation, be sure to resolve them left to right.** Thus, we first multiply 4(4) and then 3×6:

$$1 + 4(4) - 3 \times 6 \rightarrow 1 + 16 - 18$$

> Finally, we have to resolve the problem's addition and subtraction. We can do this by adding 1 and 16 and then subtracting 18 from the sum.

- Doing so proves the equation equals -1, since $17 - 18 = -1$. Because the two quantities are equal, the correct answer is (C). (If you don't remember how the answer choices work for a Quantitative Comparison question, be sure to visit section 19 of the Introduction!)

➤ Be aware, however, that **the acronym PEMDAS is a bit MISLEADING**. You don't always multiply before you divide or add before you subtract.

• In arithmetic, multiplication and division are considered EQUAL operations, as are addition and subtraction.

• Logically, this should make some sense, since division is simply multiplication by the reciprocal and subtraction is the addition of a negative number.

➤ When multiplying or dividing, be sure to **perform whichever operation comes FIRST** as you go from left to right! The same goes for addition or subtraction.

• Consider the following:

Quantity A	**Quantity B**
$4 \div 2 \times 4$	$\dfrac{1}{2}$

Answer. A. Given the order of the acronym PEMDAS, we may be tempted to conclude that the correct answer is (C).

➤ After all, if we multiply 2×4 before dividing, the two quantities appear to be equal:

$$4 \div 2 \times 4 \ \rightarrow \ 4 \div (2 \times 4) \ \rightarrow \ 4 \div 8 = \frac{4}{8} = \frac{1}{2}$$

• Unfortunately, the correct answer is not (C).

• Because multiplication and division are EQUAL operations, we MUST perform whichever operation comes first.

➤ To carry out this arithmetic correctly, we have to divide 4 by 2 BEFORE multiplying, since the division symbol precedes the multiplication symbol:

$$4 \div 2 \times 4 \ \rightarrow \ (4 \div 2) \times 4 \ \rightarrow \ 2 \times 4 = 8$$

• The correct answer is therefore (A), since Quantity A equals 8, which is greater than $\dfrac{1}{2}$.

(3) The Calculator – To reduce the emphasis on computation and to focus attention on reasoning skills, the revised GRE general test features a calculator.

• Test-takers who take the computerized version of the exam will have access to an **onscreen calculator**. Those who take the paper-based version will be provided calculators at the test center for use during the exam. **No one is allowed to bring a personal calculator.**

> ➢ The calculator has four basic functions: addition, subtraction, multiplication, and division. It also has a square root function.

• In addition to parentheses, the calculator has one memory location and three memory buttons that govern it. These buttons function as they normally do on most calculators:

The **memory sum** |M+| button inserts a number into the calculator's memory.

The **memory recall** |MR| button inserts whatever number is stored in the memory onto the calculator's display.

The **memory clear** |MC| button erases the calculator's memory so that the memory sum button can be used to store a different number.

• Onscreen, your calculator will look exactly like this:

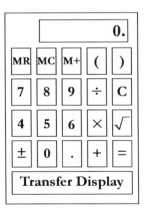

• **The Transfer Display button** can be used to transfer information from the display window of the calculator into the answer box of a Numeric Entry question.

> ➤ Although the calculator can be helpful, it is NOT NEARLY as helpful as you might imagine.

• For starters, **the onscreen calculator can be cumbersome to use**. The interface is a bit awkward, so even simple operations such as $14\ \boxed{\times}\ 15\ \boxed{\div}\ 35\ \boxed{=}$ can prove time-consuming to type.

• The awkward interface also makes it easy to mistype numbers and math symbols, which can slow you down even further.

> ➤ On average, **using the calculator will take you at least 10-20 seconds** per problem.

• If you were to use the calculator on every problem, it would consume 3-6 minutes in each of your math sections!

• That's a fairly significant chunk of time, given that each section is only 35 minutes long.

> ➤ Further, **the calculator's display screen CANNOT display more than EIGHT digits!**

• If a computation results in a number larger than 99,999,999 or smaller than 0.0000001, then "Error" will be displayed.

• For example, the calculation $10,000,000\ \boxed{\times}\ 10\ \boxed{=}$ results in "Error". The clear button $\boxed{C}$ must be used to clear the display.

> ➤ Moreover, **the calculator CANNOT handle fractions, exponents, or variables**, and it cannot store formulas.

• What's more, exam-makers can easily design problems that foil a calculator, even problems that involve such "calculator friendly" topics as multiplication or decimals!

• Consider the problem at the top of the next page:

What is the units digit of 123,456,789 × 123?

(A) 1 (B) 3 (C) 5 (D) 7 (E) 9

Answer. D. As you will learn in our chapter on Decimals, the units digit of a number is the number in its "ones column".

> ➤ In other words, it is the digit to the immediate left of the decimal. Thus, the number 453.718 has a units digit of 3 and the number 412 has a units digit of 2.

• Although our calculator can multiply 123 × 123, **it cannot multiply 123,456,789 × 123, since the product of these two numbers is greater than 99,999,999**.

• If we multiply these two numbers by hand, however, we quickly see that the correct answer must be (D), since the first row of its multiplication ends in a 7 and each subsequent row ends in one or more 0's:

$$
\begin{array}{r}
123{,}456{,}789 \\
\times \qquad 123 \\
\hline
\dots 367 \\
\dots 0 \\
+ \quad \dots 00 \\
\hline
\dots 7
\end{array}
$$

> ➤ Finally, in some problems **using a calculator can simply MISLEAD you.** Consider the following:

If $a = 6 \times 7$ and $b = 3 \times 5$, then the remainder of $a \div b = $?

(A) 0.8 (B) 4 (C) 5 (D) 8 (E) 12

Answer. E. We might be tempted to solve this problem by entering 6 × 7 into a calculator and dividing the result by 3 × 5.

• Unfortunately, not only would doing so prove more time-consuming than necessary, but it would also fail to give us the correct answer.

• Since 6 × 7 = 42 and 3 × 5 = 15, $a = 42$ and $b = 15$. When typed into a calculator, 42 ÷ 15 yields 2.8. However, neither 0.8 nor 8 is the correct answer. A remainder is the whole number left over when one number is divided by another. 42 ÷ 15 has a remainder of 12, since 15 goes into 42 two times but leaves 12 "left over", as 15 × 2 only equals 30.

- For all of these reasons, we STRONGLY encourage you **NOT to DEPEND** on the calculator.

  ➤ If you're serious about a great GRE score, you need to embrace arithmetic, not avoid it.

- As you'll see in the sections to come, many GRE problems can be solved more quickly without a calculator.

- Further, there are simple, effective strategies for every form of arithmetic that you'll encounter on the exam, and knowing them will give you insights into certain problems that a calculator cannot.

  ➤ Having said this, **there are certainly times when the calculator comes in handy**.

- While we don't want you to depend on the calculator, we DON'T want you to IGNORE it either. Particularly if your arithmetic skills are very weak.

- In the sections to come, if we present a problem or a concept in which the calculator would be beneficial for most test-takers, we will tell you.

  ➤ When using the calculator, remember that it's easy to MISTYPE entries, especially if you're in a rush.

- We encourage you to estimate your answer beforehand to determine whether the calculator's answer is "in the ballpark". This can help you avoid key-entry errors.

- During your exam, we also encourage you to **KEEP the calculator OPEN** at all times, so you don't have to click on the calculator button every time you want to use it.

(4) Time: the Hidden Topic – In many cases, the difficulty of a problem lies in the TIME you have to solve the problem, not the problem itself.

• You may understand the topic being tested but still struggle to solve the question within a respectable amount of time.

> ➢ **35 minutes for 20 problems? That's not a lot of time for any single problem.**

• And if the calculator is more often a hindrance than a source of help, what are you supposed to do?

• In a sense, you might think of time as the hidden topic tested by the GRE. It's a part of every problem – it's just not mentioned within the problem explicitly. **Improving your efficiency is a vital part of improving your GRE score.**

> ➢ There are two ways to "win the speed competition". The first is to find ways to **improve the speed of your routine calculations.**

• As you will see, there are a variety of techniques, ideas, and shortcuts – many of which you may never have been taught – that can improve the speed with which you handle numbers.

• The second way is to **know the best ways to set up and solve problems**. Most math problems can be solved in a variety of ways. Some ways, however, are dramatically superior to others.

> ➢ Knowing the best framework for a particular problem can be the difference between a 30-second solution and a 3-minute solution. Or, between **right and wrong**.

• We will help you on both fronts.

• We'll show you the arithmetic techniques and shortcuts to make you better with numbers and the proper approaches to EVERY type of GRE problem.

> ➢ To get you started, **let's look at a common trap: LONG DIVISION**. Imagine you're faced with a calculation such as $81 \div 27$ in the middle of your problem.

• Such calculations are common within many GRE problems. You might be tempted to solve it as follows:

$$27\overline{)81}^{?}$$

- In other words, you might be tempted to "guess and check" the answer.

  ➤ You might try to guess how many times 27 goes into 81 by multiplying 27 by a variety of test numbers. Does $27 \times 4 = 81$? Does $27 \times 3 = 81$?

- Vastly preferable to the "guess and check" approach (and to the calculator), would be to recognize that division can always be represented as a fraction and that fractions can be broken down like so:

$$\frac{81}{27} = \frac{9(9)}{9(3)} = 3$$

- By canceling the 9's in common to the top and bottom of the fraction, we get $\frac{9}{3} = 3$.

  ➤ In many ways, situations such as this are **the essence of GRE math: do you know a smart, simple way to solve something that looks complex**?

- With arithmetic, BREAKING numbers DOWN into manageable chunks is almost always the "smart, simple way".

- Making numbers SMALLER makes them easy to work with. Trying to work with large numbers is always a MISTAKE.

  ➤ **Large numbers are difficult to work with.** It's not easy to compute $81 \div 27$. It is easy, however, to divide 9 by 3.

- Remember, exam-makers are not interested in your ability to be a human calculator. They're interested in your ability to find smart, simple solutions to problems that seem complex.

- That's why they call the math portion of the GRE "Quantitative Reasoning". They're testing your capacity to SOLVE problems, not make them harder.

  ➤ To make numbers smaller, you simply need to break them into pieces that are easy to handle.

- **Exam-makers almost always use "smart numbers"**: numbers that are intended to simplify easily with the proper approach.

- Consider the following:

$$x = \frac{350}{14} \text{ and } y = \frac{900}{18}$$

Quantity A	Quantity B
$x + y$	70

Answer: A. We could slavishly type $350 \div 14$ into a calculator and then $900 \div 18$, but it's much faster to break these numbers down.

➤ To start, you might notice that $14 = 7 \times 2$. Can you find a way to break 350 down into $7 \times$ something? Sure: $350 = 7 \times 50$.

- Likewise, you might notice that $18 = 9 \times 2$. Can you find a way to break 900 into $9 \times$ something? Of course: $900 = 9 \times 100$. In other words, you might start this problem as follows:

$$x = \frac{350}{14} = \frac{7(50)}{7(2)} \qquad y = \frac{900}{18} = \frac{9(100)}{9(2)}$$

- In the case of x, notice that the 7's cancel, leaving $\frac{50}{2} = 25$. In the case of y, the 9's cancel, leaving $\frac{100}{2} = 50$. Thus, the correct answer is (A), since $x + y = 75$, which is greater than 70.

➤ Breaking down numbers is not only helpful with division, but it can also be helpful with multiplication.

- Let's take a look at a second sample problem:

If $a = 35 \times 5 \times 28$ and $b = 12 \times 25 \times 13$, then $\frac{a-b}{100}$ equals

(A) 6 (B) 8 (C) 9 (D) 10 (E) 12

Answer: D. When confronted with a problem such as this, **remember that exam-makers like to use smart numbers**: numbers that are intended to simplify easily under the right analysis.

➤ Further, remember that exam-makers are not interested in your ability to use the calculator.

- They are interested, however, in your ability to find a smart, quick solution to something that seems time-consuming or complex.

- Let's take a closer look at a. You might recognize that $35 = 7 \times 5$ and that $28 = 4 \times 7$. Thus, when broken down, $a = 7 \times 5 \times 5 \times 4 \times 7$.

  ➢ Further, you might also notice that some of these elements can be combined into numbers that are easy to work with.

- For example, $4 \times 5 \times 5$? That's $4 \times 25 = 100$. And the remaining 7×7? Well, that's 49. In other words, $a = 100 \times 49 = 4,900$.

- Likewise, in the case of b, you might recognize that $12 = 3 \times 4$. Thus, $b = 3 \times 4 \times 25 \times 13$.

  ➢ Notice again that some of these numbers can be combined into numbers that are easy to work with.

- 4×25? That's 100. 3×13? That's 39. And 100×39? That's $3,900$. If $a = 4,900$ and $b = 3,900$, then $a - b = 1,000$. And if $a - b = 1,000$, then $\dfrac{a-b}{100} = 10$, since:

$$\frac{a-b}{100} = \frac{1,000}{100} = 10$$

- Thus, the correct answer is (D).

  ➢ **Alternatively**, since we're dividing by 100, it can be helpful to **look** for "100's" directly.

- For example, notice that we can break a and b into the following "100's":

<u>Breaking a into 100's</u>   <u>Breaking b into 100's</u>

$$35 \times 5 \times 28 = 7 \times \underbrace{5 \times 5 \times 4}_{100} \times 7 = 49 \times 100 \qquad 12 \times 25 \times 13 = 3 \times \underbrace{4 \times 25}_{100} \times 13 = 39 \times 100$$

  ➢ As you will see in our chapter on Fractions, we can **split apart** a fraction with addition or subtraction in its **numerator**, like this:

$$\frac{a-b}{100} \rightarrow \frac{a}{100} - \frac{b}{100} \rightarrow \frac{49(\cancel{100})}{\cancel{100}} - \frac{39(\cancel{100})}{\cancel{100}}$$

- Thus, the correct answer must be (D), since $49 - 39 = 10$.

(5) Know Your Multiplication Tables – In order to break down numbers, you've got to know your multiplication tables.

• If you don't recognize the numbers involved, breaking down numbers gets a lot harder and a lot slower.

> ➤ We STRONGLY recommend that you **know your multiplication tables through 12 × 12**. (Seriously, all of the "12s"!)

• If you want to speed up your game and minimize your dependence on the calculator, you need to be able to break down numbers such as 72, 84, and 96. If you don't have your multiplication tables memorized, doing so can be difficult.

• Consider a problem like the following:

Quantity A	**Quantity B**
63 × 5 × 42	**49 × 9 × 30**

Answer: C. As always, we could attack this problem with a calculator if we had to. But if our goal is to improve our speed and save time, we ought to break down the numbers instead.

> ➤ Let's take a closer look at Quantity A. You might recognize that 63 = 7 × 9 and 42 = 6 × 7. Therefore, Quantity A equals 7 × 9 × 5 × 6 × 7.

• Likewise, in the case of Quantity B, you might recognize that 49 = 7 × 7 and 30 = 5 × 6. Thus, Quantity B equals 7 × 7 × 9 × 5 × 6.

• Thus, the correct answer is (C), since Quantity A is a product of the same numbers as Quantity B.

> ➤ When memorizing your tables, be sure to **memorize the relationships in BOTH directions**!

• It's useful to know that 6 × 9 = 54 and 7 × 12 = 84, but it's just as useful to know that 54 = 6 × 9 and 84 = 7 × 12. After all, your problem may contain numbers such as 54 and 84 that you'll need to break down.

- The multiplication table below is symmetrical. As such, **you only have to memorize HALF of it**.

  ➤ Within the table, you'll notice that every multiplication has a "twin". In some cases, you might find one twin easier to remember than the other.

- Thus, if you forget 9 × 7, you might think about 7 × 9 instead.

×	1	2	3	4	5	6	7	8	9	10	11	12
1	1	2	3	4	5	6	7	8	9	10	11	12
2	2	4	6	8	10	12	14	16	18	20	22	24
3	3	6	9	12	15	18	21	24	27	30	33	36
4	4	8	12	16	20	24	28	32	36	40	44	48
5	5	10	15	20	25	30	35	40	45	50	55	60
6	6	12	18	24	30	36	42	48	54	60	66	72
7	7	14	21	28	35	42	49	56	63	70	77	84
8	8	16	24	32	40	48	56	64	72	80	88	96
9	9	18	27	36	45	54	63	72	81	90	99	108
10	10	20	30	40	50	60	70	80	90	100	110	120
11	11	22	33	44	55	66	77	88	99	110	121	132
12	12	24	36	48	60	72	84	96	108	120	132	144

- Down the middle, you'll notice a diagonal line of "PERFECT SQUARES" that cuts the table in two. Perfect squares are numbers such as 25 = 5 × 5, 64 = 8 × 8, and 121 = 11 × 11.

- If you know your perfect squares, there's a math trick that you may find handy:

  ➤ To multiply two numbers separated by 2 (such as 5 × 7), **SUBTRACT one from the SQUARE of the number BETWEEN them.**

- For example:

  5 × 7 = 35, since 6 is between them and 6 × 6 = 36
  11 × 13 = 143, since 12 is between them and 12 × 12 = 144
  14 × 16 = 224, since 15 is between them and 15 × 15 = 225
  19 × 21 = 399, since 20 is between them and 20 × 20 = 400

(6) Squares, Cubes, and Special Powers – To further improve your ability to break down numbers, it can also help to memorize a short list of squares, cubes, and special powers.

• As with multiplication tables, doing so will help you solve certain problems far more quickly!

1. **Squares & Cubes**

• As we've seen, a perfect square is a number such as $25 = 5 \times 5 = 5^2$. A perfect cube is a number such as $8 = 2 \times 2 \times 2 = 2^3$ or $64 = 4 \times 4 \times 4 = 4^3$.

> ➤ **Be sure to learn the following lists in both directions!** In fact, it's generally more useful to know that $225 = 15^2$ or $64 = 4^3$ than it is to know that $15^2 = 225$ or $4^3 = 64$.

• And remember: a square root is the "opposite" of a square and **a cube root is the "opposite of a cube"**. Thus, if $25^2 = 625$ and $4^3 = 64$, then $\sqrt{625} = 25$ and $\sqrt[3]{64} = 4$.

Squares	
$10^2 = 100$	$15^2 = 225$
$11^2 = 121$	$20^2 = 400$
$12^2 = 144$	$25^2 = 625$
$13^2 = 169$	$30^2 = 900$
$14^2 = 196$	

Cubes	
$1^3 = 1$	$5^3 = 125$
$2^3 = 8$	$6^3 = 216$
$3^3 = 27$	$10^3 = 1,000$
$4^3 = 64$	

2. **Special Powers.**

• Many GRE problems involve the powers of 2, 3, 4, and 5. As with squares and cubes, it can be useful to **learn these lists in both directions.** It's just as useful to know that $4^4 = 256$ as it is to know that $256 = 4^4$.

Special Powers: 2, 3, 4, & 5			
$2^1 = 2$	$3^1 = 3$	$4^1 = 4$	$5^1 = 5$
$2^2 = 4$	$3^2 = 9$	$4^2 = 16$	$5^2 = 25$
$2^3 = 8$	$3^3 = 27$	$4^3 = 64$	$5^3 = 125$
$2^4 = 16$	$3^4 = 81$	$4^4 = 256$	$5^4 = 625$
$2^5 = 32$	$3^5 = 243$		
$2^6 = 64$			

(7) Square Roots from 1 to 10 – GRE problems often involve the roots from $\sqrt{1}$ to $\sqrt{10}$. In fact, they show up more than you might expect.

• Geometry, for example, often features such roots, since certain right triangles contain legs with root values.

➤ As you will learn, the legs of a right isosceles triangle and of a 30°– 60°– 90° right triangle always have the following dimensions:

Right Isosceles   **30–60°–90°**

$x : x : x\sqrt{2}$ $x : x\sqrt{3} : 2x$

• When working with these roots, it will save you time to have the following values memorized:

$$\sqrt{1} = 1 \qquad \sqrt{2} \approx 1.4 \qquad \sqrt{3} \approx 1.7 \qquad \sqrt{4} = 2 \qquad \sqrt{5} \approx 2.2$$
$$\sqrt{6} \approx 2.4 \qquad \sqrt{7} \approx 2.6 \qquad \sqrt{8} \approx 2.8 \qquad \sqrt{9} = 3 \qquad \sqrt{10} \approx 3.2$$

The "≈" symbol means "approximately".

• An easy way to do so is to remember that values larger than $\sqrt{4}$ **increase in increments of 0.2**, and values smaller than $\sqrt{4}$ **decrease in increments of 0.3**.

Greater than $\sqrt{4}$: Add 0.2   **Less than $\sqrt{4}$: Subtract 0.3**

$\sqrt{4} = 2$ $\sqrt{4} = 2$

$\sqrt{5} \approx 2.2$ $\sqrt{3} \approx 1.7$

$\sqrt{6} \approx 2.4$ $\sqrt{2} \approx 1.4$

$\sqrt{7} \approx 2.6$

$\sqrt{8} \approx 2.8$

$\sqrt{9} = 3$

$\sqrt{10} \approx 3.2$

➤ This pattern doesn't hold forever. For example, $\sqrt{11}$ is closer to 3.5 than to 3.4 and $\sqrt{1}$ is not 1.1. It does hold, however, for the square roots from 2 to 10.

• To understand how these values can save you time, consider the following sample problem:

Quantity A	Quantity B
$\sqrt{2} + \sqrt{6} + \sqrt{8}$	4

Answer. A. At this point in your preparation, you may not know the rules of roots, so like many test-takers, you may be tempted to add the roots in Quantity A as follows:

$$\sqrt{2} + \sqrt{6} + \sqrt{8} \quad \rightarrow \quad \sqrt{16} = 4$$

➢ Unfortunately, **this is a trap question: it's been designed to take advantage of a common misunderstanding.**

• Roots CANNOT be added in this manner, as you will learn when we discuss the properties of roots with you. On the contrary, we know that:

$$\sqrt{2} \approx 1.4 \qquad \sqrt{6} \approx 2.4 \qquad \sqrt{8} \approx 2.8$$

• Since 1.4 + 2.4 + 2.8 add to something much larger than 4 (**don't waste your time adding numbers you don't have to!**), the correct answer must be (A).

(8) Fraction to Decimal Equivalents: the "Conversion List" – Many GRE questions require the conversion of fractions to decimals.

- Other questions may require you to recognize the fractional equivalent of a decimal.

  ➢ Both tasks will be dramatically easier and faster if you memorize the following values.

- From here on, these values will be referred to as the "Conversion List".

$$\frac{1}{2} = 0.5 \qquad \frac{1}{5} = 0.2 \qquad \frac{1}{8} = 0.125 \qquad \frac{1}{11} = 0.\overline{09}$$

$$\frac{1}{3} = 0.\overline{3} \qquad \frac{1}{6} = 0.1\overline{6} \qquad \frac{1}{9} = 0.\overline{1} \qquad \frac{1}{99} = 0.\overline{01}$$

$$\frac{1}{4} = 0.25 \qquad \frac{1}{7} \approx 0.14 \qquad \frac{1}{10} = 0.1 \qquad \frac{1}{100} = 0.01$$

The "≈" symbol means "approximately"

- According to the "Conversion List", $\frac{1}{5} = 0.2$. Thus, the decimal value of $\frac{2}{5}$ is 0.4, since $\frac{2}{5}$ is twice as big as $\frac{1}{5}$.

  ➢ Likewise, since $\frac{1}{8} = 0.125$, the decimal value of $\frac{3}{8}$ is 0.375, since $\frac{3}{8}$ is three times as big as $\frac{1}{8}$.

- Conversely, if $\frac{1}{7} \approx 0.14$, then the fractional value of 0.28 must approximately equal $\frac{2}{7}$, since 0.28 is twice as big as 0.14.

- Likewise, if $\frac{1}{4} = 0.25$, then the fractional value of 0.255 should approximately equal $\frac{1}{4}$, since 0.255 ≈ 0.25.

  ➢ To get a sense of how the "Conversion List" can save you time on the GRE, let's work through a practice problem together.

- Consider the following:

What is the 16th digit to the right of the decimal point in the decimal equivalent of $\frac{3}{11}$?

(A) 1   (B) 3   (C) 5   (D) 7   (E) 9

Answer. D. According to our "conversion list", $\frac{1}{11} = 0.\overline{09}$.

• The bar over the .09 indicates that those digits repeat forever: 0.090909… Likewise, the notation $0.\overline{3}$ represents the decimal 0.3333…, while the notation $0.1\overline{6}$ represents the decimal 0.16666…

➢ The fraction $\frac{3}{11}$ indicates that we have "three 11ths", in the same way that the fraction $\frac{2}{3}$ indicates that we have "two 3rds".

• So if $\frac{1}{11} = 0.\overline{09}$, then $\frac{3}{11}$ must equal 3 times that amount. Similarly, if $\frac{1}{3} = 0.\overline{3}$, then $\frac{2}{3}$ must equal 2 times that amount.

• As you will learn when we formally cover decimals, $0.09 \times 3 = 0.27$. Thus, $0.\overline{09} \times 3 = 0.\overline{27}$.

➢ Since $0.\overline{27} = 0.272727…$, and every <u>even-placed</u> digit to the right of the decimal point is a "7", the 16th digit (an <u>even-placed</u> digit) must also be a "7".

• The correct answer is therefore (D).

Arithmetic Shortcuts

(9) The "Multiplication Trick" – Throughout this section, we've introduced several concepts and number lists to help you work with numbers more quickly and easily.

• We now want to focus on a few math shortcuts to complement that material. Before we get started, however, a small note: these ideas might come with a small learning curve.

➢ The familiar techniques that they'll replace have been with you for years, so it may take you a little bit of practice before they truly make you faster.

• Stick with them! They will definitely improve the speed of your calculations once you internalize them.

• The first of these shortcuts is something we call the "Multiplication Trick". This technique is helpful because it allows us to multiply difficult numbers easily. Here's how it works:

➢ **When multiplying by something complicated,** see if you can split that number into TWO parts that are LESS complicated.

• For example, 9(21) is much easier to work with if we split the 21 into 20 + 1, since it's easy to multiply 9(20) and 9(1). Thus:

$$9(20 + 1) = 9(20) + 9(1) = 180 + 9 = 189$$

• Likewise, 12(12.5) is much easier to work with if we split the 12.5 into 12 + 0.5, since it's easy to multiply 12(12) and 12(0.5). Thus:

$$12(12 + 0.5) = 12(12) + 12(0.5) = 144 + 6 = 150$$

➢ On occasion, the GRE will test this concept directly, but in the opposite direction. Here's an example:

Quantity A	**Quantity B**
241 × 11.6	**241(11) + 241(0.6)**

Answer: C. The quantities must be equal, since 241 × 11.6 can be broken down as:

$$241(11 + 0.6) = 241(11) + 241(0.6)$$

(10) Chunking: the Division Shortcut – Another useful shortcut is a technique commonly known as "Chunking".

- Chunking is an alternative way of DIVIDING numbers.

  ➢ It's particularly effective on the GRE, since exam-makers almost always use smart numbers: numbers designed to yield easily to proper analysis.

- Chunking works by breaking numbers into **"manageable chunks"**. Imagine that you wanted to divide 168 by 14. You might notice that 140 is easily divisible by 14. (A multiple of 10 is often a good first "chunk".)

- If you were to break 168 into "chunks" of 140 and 28, you could easily divide each of these chunks by 14. Thus, $168 \div 14$ equals $\boxed{12}$, since $140 \div 14 = \boxed{10}$ and $28 \div 14 = \boxed{2}$.

  ➢ Likewise, imagine that you wanted to divide 165 by 11. You might notice that 110 is easily divisible by 11.

- If you were to break 165 into "chunks" of 110 and 55, you could easily divide each of these chunks by 11. Thus, $165 \div 11$ equals $\boxed{15}$, since $110 \div 11 = \boxed{10}$ and $55 \div 11 = \boxed{5}$.

- Chunking works just as easily if there's a remainder.

  ➢ Imagine that you wanted to divide 108 by 7. You might notice that 70 is easily divisible by 7.

- If you were to break 108 into "chunks" of 70 and 38, you could easily divide each of these chunks by 7. Thus, $108 \div 7$ equals $\boxed{15 \text{ rem. } 3}$, since $70 \div 7 = \boxed{10}$ and $38 \div 7 = \boxed{5 \text{ rem. } 3}$.

  ➢ Likewise, imagine that you wanted to divide 142 by 3. You might notice that 120 is easily divisible by 3.

- If you were to break 142 into "chunks" of 120 and 22, you could easily divide each of these chunks by 3. Thus, $142 \div 3$ equals $\boxed{47 \text{ rem. } 1}$, since $120 \div 3 = \boxed{40}$ and $22 \div 3 = \boxed{7 \text{ rem. } 1}$.

(11) Number Tricks – In addition to the "Multiplication Trick" and "Chunking", there are several number tricks that can improve the speed of your computations.

- We encourage you to learn them as quickly as possible.

  ➢ Many GRE questions demand the ability to multiply or divide by numbers such as 4, 5, 8, 9, and 11, or to add numbers such as 18 + 35.

- If you can do so easily, you can save yourself a lot of time.

- The first of these tricks involves | **Multiplying and Dividing by 4 and 8** |. To understand how this trick works, imagine that you wanted to multiply 25 × 12.

  ➢ Because 12 = 4 × 3, you could multiply 25 first by 4 and then by 3 to get the same result. Hence, 25 × 12 = 300, since 25 × 4 = 100 and 100 × 3 = 300.

- Likewise, imagine that you wanted to divide 120 by 15. Because 15 = 3 × 5, you could divide 120 first by 3 and then by 5 (or by 5 and then by 3) to get the same result.

- Thus, 120 ÷ 15 = 8, since 120 ÷ 3 = 40 and 40 ÷ 5 = 8.

  ➢ This trick is particularly helpful for multiplying and dividing by 4 and 8, since 4 and 8 are composed solely of "twos", and doubling and halving numbers is fairly easy to do.

- For example, 4 = 2 × 2. Therefore, to multiply or divide a number by 4, we simply need to DOUBLE or HALVE it TWICE:

Multiply by 4	Divide by 4
13 × 4: 13 → 26 → 52	56 ÷ 4: 56 → 28 → 14
16 × 4: 16 → 32 → 64	72 ÷ 4: 72 → 36 → 18

- Similarly, 8 = 2 × 2 × 2, so to multiply or divide a number by 8, we only need to DOUBLE or HALVE it THREE times:

Multiply by 8	Divide by 8
12 × 8: 12 → 24 → 48 → 96	120 ÷ 8: 120 → 60 → 30 → 15
16 × 8: 16 → 32 → 64 → 128	144 ÷ 8: 144 → 72 → 36 → 18

- Our next number trick involves **Multiplying by 9, 11, and 99**.

  ➢ Imagine that you wanted to multiply a number by 9. Since $9 = 10 - 1$, you could MULTIPLY by 10 instead and SUBTRACT the original number to get the same result:

- Likewise, if you wanted to MULTIPLY by 11, you could multiply by 10 and then ADD the original number, since $11 = 10 + 1$:

Multiply by 9	Multiply by 11
14×9: $(14 \times 10) - 14 = 140 - 14 = 126$	14×11: $(14 \times 10) + 14 = 140 + 14 = 154$
23×9: $(23 \times 10) - 23 = 230 - 23 = 207$	23×11: $(23 \times 10) + 23 = 230 + 23 = 253$

- Similarly, if you wanted to MULTIPLY by 99, you could multiply by 100 and then SUBTRACT the original number, since $99 = 100 - 1$:

Multiply by 99
5×99: $(5 \times 100) - 5 = 500 - 5 = 495$
8×99: $(8 \times 100) - 8 = 800 - 8 = 792$

  ➢ One particularly useful number trick involves **Multiplying and Dividing by 5**.

- Because $5 = 10 \div 2$, you can MULTIPLY a number by 10 and THEN divide that answer by 2 (or divide it by 2 and then multiply that answer by 10) to get the same result as multiplying it by 5:

Multiply by 5
14×5: $(14 \times 10) \div 2 = 140 \div 2 = 70$
18×5: $(18 \times 10) \div 2 = 180 \div 2 = 90$

- Likewise, to DIVIDE by 5, you can DIVIDE a number by 10 and THEN multiply that answer by 2 (or multiply it by 2 and then divide that answer by 10), since division is the inverse of multiplication:

Divide by 5
$80 \div 5$: $(80 \div 10) \times 2 = 8 \times 2 = 16$
$92 \div 5$: $(92 \div 10) \times 2 = 9.2 \times 2 = 18.4$

(12) The Addition Shortcut – There are also some great number tricks for ADDING and SUBTRACTING numbers.

- We call the first of these tricks the "Addition Shortcut".

  ➢ The shortcut works by adding the tens digits and the units digits of a set of numbers SEPARATELY.

- To get a sense of how it works, let's add 47 + 38.

- Rather than stacking the numbers atop one another, adding the columns, and potentially "carrying" digits, first IGNORE the units digits. This gives you 40 + 30 = $\boxed{70}$.

  ➢ Then add the units digits. This gives you 7 + 8 = $\boxed{15}$. Since 70 + 15 = 85, the sum of 47 + 38 is therefore $\boxed{85}$.

- Visually, you can think of the process like this:

$$
\begin{array}{c|c}
4 & 7 \\
+\ 3 & 8 \\
\hline
\end{array}
$$

These numbers equal 40 + 30 = 70

These numbers equal 7 + 8 = 15

  ➢ Likewise, to add 23 + 35 + 51, all we have to do is add 20 + 30 + 50 = $\boxed{100}$ and then add 3 + 5 + 1 = $\boxed{9}$.

- Since 100 + 9 = 109, the sum of 23 + 35 + 51 is therefore $\boxed{109}$:

$$
\begin{array}{c|c}
2 & 3 \\
3 & 5 \\
+\ 5 & 1 \\
\hline
\end{array}
$$

These numbers equal 20 + 30 + 50 = 100

These numbers equal 3 + 5 + 1 = 9

  ➢ A final example for you: to add 38 + 43 + 52, we simply have to add 30 + 40 + 50 = $\boxed{120}$ and then add 8 + 3 + 2 = $\boxed{13}$.

- Since 120 + 13 = 133, the sum of 38 + 43 + 52 is therefore $\boxed{133}$.

(13) Subtraction by Addition – Our subtraction shortcut works by using addition in place of subtraction.

- Imagine that you needed to subtract 123 – 87.

  ➢ One way you could do so would be to picture BOTH values on a NUMBER LINE with a SIMPLE point, such as 100, somewhere between them.

- As you can see in the diagram below, 87 is 13 "spaces" from 100 and 100 is 23 "spaces" from 123:

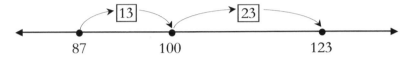

- Thus, the difference between 87 and 123 equals $\boxed{13}$ + $\boxed{23}$, or 36, since the difference between two numbers is simply the DISTANCE between them on the number line.

  ➢ Of course, you don't really need to draw a number line to subtract numbers with this strategy.

- For example, if you needed to subtract 86 – 29, you could choose a simple number BETWEEN them, such as 50, and ask yourself:

  1. "What is the distance from 29 to 50?" 21.
  2. "What is the distance from 50 to 86?" 36.

- The answer would therefore be 57, since $\boxed{21}$ + $\boxed{36}$ = 57.

  ➢ To ensure that you've got it, let's work through one more example together. Say you needed to subtract 211 – 83.

- To start, you would need to choose a simple number between 211 and 83, such as 100.

- From there, you need would to calculate the distance from 83 to 100, which is 17, and then the distance from 100 to 211, which is 111. Thus, the answer would be 128, since $\boxed{17}$ + $\boxed{111}$ = 128.

➤ Alternatively, you can subtract numbers such as 139 − 86 by asking yourself one question: "86 + WHAT number gets me CLOSE to 139?"

• In some cases, your estimate might take you to a value a little BELOW your target.

• For example, if you were to guess 50 here, notice that 86 + 50 takes you to 136, which is three LESS than 139. Thus, you'd need to ADD three to your estimate, making $\boxed{50} + \boxed{3}$, or 53, the correct answer.

➤ In other cases, your estimate might take you to a value a little ABOVE your target.

• For example, if you needed to subtract 83 − 39, you might estimate that 39 + 50 gets you close to 83.

• Notice, however, that 39 + 50 = 89, which is six MORE than 83. Thus, you'd need to SUBTRACT six from your estimate, making $\boxed{50} - \boxed{6}$, or 44, the correct answer.

➤ To ensure that you've got it, let's work through one more example together. Imagine that you needed to subtract 167 − 49.

• To start, you would ask yourself: "49 + WHAT gets me close to 167?" From there, you would estimate a value, such as 120.

• Because 49 + 120 takes you to 169, which is two MORE than 167, you'd need to SUBTRACT two from your estimate, making $\boxed{120} - \boxed{2}$, or 118, the correct answer.

➤ It doesn't matter to us whether you prefer this strategy or the one on the previous page. We encourage you, however, to embrace at least one of them.

• Many GRE problems involve subtraction. Having a strategy that allows you to subtract quickly will save you time on each of those problems.

(14) Quick Percents: the "10% Shortcut" – Percents are another great place to use shortcuts.

• If you can get 10% of a number, you can get other percents of that number (e.g. 5%, 15%, 20%, 30%, etc.) very easily.

➤ To get 10% of a number, simply SLIDE its decimal spot ONE space to the left:

$$10\% \text{ of } 82 = 8.2 \qquad 10\% \text{ of } 230 = 23 \qquad 10\% \text{ of } 0.05 = 0.005$$

• To get 5% of a number, therefore, simply take HALF of 10%:

$$5\% \text{ of } 270 = \frac{1}{2} \text{ of } 27 = 13.5 \qquad 5\% \text{ of } 38 = \frac{1}{2} \text{ of } 3.8 = 1.9$$

• Similarly, to get 15% of a number, ADD 10% and 5% together:

$$15\% \text{ of } 220 = 10\% + 5\% = 22 + \left(\frac{1}{2} \text{ of } 22\right) = 22 + 11 = 33$$

• Likewise, to get 20%, 30%, or 40% of a number, get 10% of that number and double, triple, or quadruple it.

$$20\% \text{ of } 180 = 10\% \times 2 = 18 \times 2 = 36 \qquad 60\% \text{ of } 110 = 10\% \times 6 = 11 \times 6 = 66$$

➤ If you can get 1% of a number, this technique can also be used to determine more complicated percents, such as 6%, 11%, or 99%.

• To get 1% of a number, simply SLIDE its decimal spot TWO spaces to the left:

$$1\% \text{ of } 82 = 0.82 \qquad 1\% \text{ of } 230 = 2.3 \qquad 1\% \text{ of } 0.05 = 0.0005$$

• Thus, to get 6% of a number, add 5% and 1% together:

$$6\% \text{ of } 120 = 5\% + 1\% = \frac{1}{2} \text{ of } 12 + 1.2 = 6 + 1.2 = 7.2$$

• Likewise, to get 31% of a number, add 30% and 1% together:

$$31\% \text{ of } 40 = (10\% \times 3) + 1\% = (4 \times 3) + 0.4 = 12.4$$

• In general, you SHOULDN'T need to determine 1% of a number very often (if at all). Still, it can come in handy every now and then. As always, just be sure that you're not missing an easier approach before using it!

(15) The Divisibility Rules – From time to time, you may come across numbers that lie outside your comfort zone.

• A small list of rules, commonly known as the Divisibility Rules, can help you determine whether these "uncomfortable" numbers are divisible by frequently used smaller numbers, such as those from 2 to 10.

  ➢ The rules for 5 and 10 are very simple.

Number	An integer is divisible by 5 or 10 …
5	If it ends in a 0 or a 5.
10	If it ends in a 0.

• Thus, numbers such as 130 and 285 are divisible by 5, since they end in a 0 or a 5. Likewise, 170 is divisible by 10, since it ends in a 0.

  ➢ The rules for 2, 4, and 8 are similar to one another.

Number	An integer is divisible by 2, 4, or 8 …
2	If its <u>last</u> digit can be cut in half <u>once</u>.
4	If its last <u>two</u> digits can be cut in half <u>twice</u>.
8	If its last <u>three</u> digits can be cut in half <u>thrice</u>.

• Hence, 116 is divisible by 2, as its last digit can be cut in half once: $6 \rightarrow 3$. 228 is divisible by 4, as its last two digits can be cut in half twice: $28 \rightarrow 14 \rightarrow 7$. And 4,200 is divisible by 8, as its last three digits can be cut in half three times: $200 \rightarrow 100 \rightarrow 50 \rightarrow 25$.

  ➢ The rules for 3 and 9 are also similar to one another.

Number	An integer is divisible by 3 or 9 …
3	If the sum of its digits is divisible by $\boxed{3}$.
9	If the sum of its digits is divisible by $\boxed{9}$.

• Thus, 381 is divisible by 3, since $3 + 8 + 1 = 12$, which is divisible by 3. Likewise, 738 is divisible by 3, since $7 + 3 + 8 = 18$, which is divisible by 9.

➤ The rule for 6 is a composite of the rules for 2 and 3, since 6 = 2 × 3.

Number	An integer is divisible by 6 …
6	If it's divisible by 2 and by 3 .

• Hence, 108 is divisible by 6, since its last digit can be cut in half (the "2" rule) and the sum of its digits add to 9, which is divisible by 3 (the "3" rule).

➤ Finally, to determine whether a number is divisible by 7, "chunk" it. Although there is a rule for 7, it's more time-consuming than chunking.

• Remember, this is all in an effort to increase your efficiency! Thus, 224 is divisible by 7, since we can break 224 into 210 + 14, and each of these "chunks" is divisible by 7.

• In short, the Rules of Divisibility can be summarized as follows:

2	If the last digit can be cut in half once.	116 is. 117 is not.
3	If the sum of the digits is divisible by 3.	381 is, since $3+8+1=12$. 385 is not, since $3+8+5=16$.
4	If the last two digits can be cut in half twice.	228 is, since $28 \rightarrow 14 \rightarrow 7$. 282 is not, since $82 \rightarrow 41 \rightarrow 20.5$
5	If the integer ends in a 0 or 5.	75 is. 84 is not.
6	If the integer is divisible by 2 and 3.	108 is, since 8 is even and $1+0+8=9$. 117 is not, since the last digit is odd.
8	If the last three digits can be cut in half thrice.	104 is, since $104 \rightarrow 52 \rightarrow 26 \rightarrow 13$. 124 is not, since $124 \rightarrow 62 \rightarrow 31 \rightarrow 15.5$.
9	If the sum of the digits is divisible by 9.	738 is, since $7+3+8=18$. 743 is not, since $7+4+3=14$.
10	If the integer ends in a 0.	70 is. 75 is not.

➤ To get a sense of how these rules can help, let's work through a couple of practice problems together.

• Consider the following:

Which of the following is a factor of 5,427?

(A) 4   (B) 5   (C) 6   (D) 7   (E) 9

Answer. E. The term "factor" refers to a small number that divides cleanly into a larger number. For example, 7 is a factor of 28, since 7 divides cleanly into 28.

> Since **an integer is divisible by 9 if the sum of its digits is divisible by 9**, the number 5,427 must be divisible by 9: its digits add to $5 + 4 + 2 + 7 = 18$.

- The correct answer is therefore (E).

The number 10^{15} is divisible by all of the following EXCEPT

(A) 500   (B) 250   (C) 64   (D) 32   (E) 6

Answer. E. While there are several ways to solve this question, one easy way to do so is with the divisibility rules.

- As you will learn in our chapter on Decimals, the exponent of a power of 10 indicates the number of zeroes that trail the initial "1".

> Thus, 10^{15} equals **a "1" followed by fifteen zeroes**.

- A number is divisible by 6 if it is divisible by 2 <u>and</u> 3, and a number is divisible by 3 if the sum of its digits is divisible by 3.

- Because the digits of 1,000,000,000,000,000 add to 1, the sum of its digits is NOT divisible by 3. Since 10^{15} is not divisible by 3, it is not divisible by 6, either. The correct answer must therefore be (E).

Chapter 2: Arithmetic

Practice Questions

(16) Problem Sets – The shortcuts covered in this chapter may come with a small learning curve.

- They'll be replacing familiar techniques that have been with you for years, so it will take practice before they make you faster. Stick with them!

  ➢ Once internalized, they will improve the speed of your calculations and save you valuable minutes over the course of your exam.

- Remember, each of your quantitative sections will have 20 questions. Your arithmetic skills will affect almost every one.

- If you can save 10-20 seconds per question by enhancing those skills, you will save anywhere between 3 and 7 minutes per section. For most test-takers, an extra 3 to 7 minutes is the difference between completing the sections and guessing to beat the clock!

Drills

1. Answer each of the following by breaking down the numbers:

   (a) Does $16 \times 25 = 400$? (b) Does $18 \times 9 = 162$?
   (c) Does $14 \times 35 = 500$? (d) Does $35 \times 15 \times 12 = 6,300$?

2. For each of the following, find the fractional or decimal equivalent without using a calculator or long division:

   (a) $\frac{2}{7}$ (b) $\frac{4}{9}$
   (c) $0.\overline{5}$ (d) 0.375
   (e) $\frac{3}{11}$ (f) $\frac{5}{99}$

3. For each of the following, find a numerical equivalent without using a calculator. Some may have more than one answer:

   (a) $\sqrt{2}$ (b) $\sqrt{7}$
   (c) 15^2 (d) 5^3
   (e) 16 (f) 64

4. Use the "multiplication trick" to answer each of the following:

   (a) 8(17)   (b) 11(14)
   (c) 31(13)   (d) 7(123)

5. Calculate each of the following with a "number trick":

   (a) 16×9 (b) 21×11
   (c) 7×99 (d) 14×16

6. Use a "number trick" to determine each of the following:

   (a) $90 \div 5$ (b) $92 \div 4$
   (c) $144 \div 8$ (d) $210 \div 6$

7. Find the sum for each of the following with the "addition shortcut":

   (a) 47 + 75   (b) 93 + 89
   (c) 23 + 54 + 38   (d) 42 + 33 + 57

8. Use our "subtraction by addition" shortcut to calculate the following:

   (a) 63 – 27   (b) 81 – 39
   (c) 123 – 64   (d) 231 – 87

9. Use "chunking" to answer each of the following:

   (a) $165 \div 3$ (b) $108 \div 9$
   (c) $322 \div 14$ (d) $255 \div 11$

10. Calculate each of the following with the "10% shortcut":

    (a) 5%, 10%, and 15% of 40   (b) 20%, 40%, and 60% of 120
    (c) 1%, 10%, and 12% of 240   (d) 1%, 10%, and 98% of 110

11. Use the "divisibility rules" to answer each of the following:

    (a) Is 189 divisible by 3 and 9?   (b) Is 480 divisible by 3, 6, and 9?
    (c) Is 108 divisible by 3, 4, 6, and 9? (d) Is 405 divisible by 3, 5, and 9?

Questions

	Quantity A	Quantity B

12. 233.104(5.005)   5(233.104) + 0.005(233.104)

13. What is the lowest positive integer that is divisible by each of the integers 1 through 8, inclusive?

(A) 420   (B) 840   (C) 1,260   (D) 2,520   (E) 5,040

	Quantity A	Quantity B

14. The 30th digit to the right of the decimal point in the decimal equivalent of $\frac{18}{99}$?   The 41st digit to the right of the decimal point in the decimal equivalent of $\frac{18}{99}$?

15. Which of the following are divisors of 396?

Select all such values.

A 4   B 6   C 7   D 9   E 11   F 18

$$x = 30 \times 32 \times 33 \times 35 \times 36 \times 39$$

	Quantity A	Quantity B

16. The product of every integer from 1 to 13 $4x$

	Quantity A	Quantity B

17. $\sqrt{3} + \sqrt[3]{3} + \sqrt[4]{3}$ 5.1

18. $81 \times 42 \times 35 \times 30 \times 16$ is most nearly equal to which of the following?

(A) 4^7 (B) 5^8 (C) 7^8 (D) 6^{10} (E) 9^{11}

(17) Solutions – Video solutions for each of the previous questions can be found on our website at **www.sherpaprep.com/videos**.

- BOOKMARK this address for future visits!

  ➤ To view the videos, you'll need the LOGIN and PASSWORD that you created upon registering your copy of <u>Arithmetic & "Plan B" Strategies</u>.

- If you have yet to register your book yet, please go to **www.sherpaprep.com/activate** and enter your email address, last name, and shipping address.

- Be sure to provide the SAME last name and shipping address that you used to purchase your copy of <u>Master Key to the GRE</u> or to enroll in your GRE course with Sherpa Prep!

  ➤ When checking your answers, we encourage you to watch the solution for any problem that you answered INCORRECTLY

- The same goes for any problem that took you MORE than TWO MINUTES to solve.

- After digesting the explanation, REVISIT your mistake a couple of days later to ensure that the problem no longer poses issues to you.

  ➤ If you struggle to solve the problem a SECOND time, add it to your "LOG of ERRORS" and redo it every few weeks.

- Solving tricky questions MORE THAN ONCE is the best way to learn from your mistakes and to avoid similar difficulties on your actual exam.

Drill 1	Drill 2
a. Yes.	a. Approximately 0.28
b. Yes.	b. $0.\overline{4}$
c. No. $14 \times 35 = 490$	c. 5/9
d. Yes.	d. 3/8
	e. $0.\overline{27}$
	f. $0.0\overline{5}$

Drill 3

a. Approximately 1.4
b. Approximately 2.6
c. 225
d. 125
e. 4^2 and 2^4
f. 8^2, 4^3, and 2^6

Drill 5

a. 144
b. 231
c. 693
d. 224

Drill 7

a. 122
b. 182
c. 115
d. 132

Drill 9

a. 55
b. 12
c. 23
d. 23 rem. 2

Drill 4

a. 136
b. 154
c. 403
d. 861

Drill 6

a. 18
b. 23
c. 18
d. 35

Drill 8

a. 36
b. 42
c. 59
d. 144

Drill 10

a. 2, 4, and 6
b. 24, 48, and 72
c. 2.4, 24, and 28.8
d. 1.1, 11, 107.8

Drill 11

a. Yes.

b. Only by 3 and by 6.

c. Yes.

d. Yes.

Practice Questions

12. C

13. B

14. A

15. A, B, D, E, and F

16. C

17. B

18. D

Chapter 3

"Plan B" Strategies

"Plan B" Strategies

To be discussed:

Smart Math

Our first group of strategies contains tips for avoiding difficult or time-consuming arithmetic.

Using the Answers

The following sections will show you how to use the answer choices to your advantage.

Picking Numbers

Picking numbers is a great way of turning confusing, abstract problems into simple, less intimidating ones.

Guess Strategies

Our final group of "Plan B" strategies is a small collection of tips for guessing.

Practice Questions

Practice your new skills to ensure that you internalize what you've studied.

Smart Math

(1) Introduction – Over the course of your exam, you will likely come across problems that you struggle to solve.

• Some of these problems may involve a wrinkle you find confusing, others may involve concepts that are unfamiliar to you. In some cases, you may simply draw a blank on material you know well.

➤ Well, there's good news. There are a variety of tricks, tips, and techniques – we call them "Plan B" strategies – that can bail you out of such situations.

• As the name "Plan B" suggests, you may not want to make these strategies your first plan of attack, especially if you understand the content of your question.

• However, **these strategies are a healthy complement to knowing how to do things the "right way".**

➤ We encourage you to embrace them. Not only can they help you out of a jam, but they're also quick, fast, and effective.

• In fact, these strategies can sometimes help you solve problems more quickly than doing so the "right way". And with <u>certain</u> problem types, these strategies may be the key to solving the problem the "right way".

• That said, these strategies can only take you so far.

➤ Although they can be extremely effective with certain problems, **they are not a substitute for knowing how to solve problems the "right way".**

• They cannot help you achieve a great GRE score on their own, so do not become dependent on them.

• <u>Master Key to the GRE</u> will teach you simple ways to solve <u>every</u> type of GRE question efficiently. **Be sure to learn them properly**! If you use our "Plan B" strategies to back up what you learn, you will have the perfect complement of knowledge and strategy.

Chapter 3: "Plan B" Strategies

(2) "Time Suck" Problems – In general, our "Plan B" strategies fall into four general groups.

• The first of these groups contains "smart" strategies for avoiding difficult or time-consuming arithmetic.

> ➤ Every GRE exam contains at least one example (and usually more) of what we call "Time Suck" problems.

• "Time Suck" problems are designed **to bait test-takers into performing a large number of math steps or calculations**. The steps or calculations are usually easy to perform, but are typically time-consuming.

• Thus, many test-takers answer such problems correctly, but waste a lot of time doing so.

> ➤ Remember, **test makers are not interested in your ability to perform a series of tedious calculations** or to use their awkward calculator.

• They're interested in your ability to find a smart, quick solution to something that seems time-consuming or complex.

• When faced with a question that seems to require a LOT of busy work, always step back from the problem and ask yourself "**Am I missing something?**" In some cases you may not, but in many cases you likely are. Consider the following:

What is the value of 17(18) + 19(17) + 17(20) + 21(17) + 17(22)?

(A) 1,200   (B) 1,440   (C) 1,700   (D) 1,840   (E) 2,100

Answer: C. To solve this problem, we may be tempted to multiply each term in the question and to add their sums.

> ➤ To do so, however, would involve a series of tedious calculations. We can certainly do them, but it would be time-consuming.

• In such cases, we should always ask ourselves "Am I missing something?" In this problem, there is definitely a better alternative than to multiply all these terms individually.

➤ Notice that **each term in the question involves the number 17**. To solve this problem quickly, we simply need to factor that 17 from each of its terms.

• As you will learn when we cover Algebra with you, the term "factoring" refers to the removal of the greatest element common to two or more terms.

• If we remove 17 from each of the terms in the question, we get:

$$17(18 + 19 + 20 + 21 + 22)$$

➤ To solve this question, then, all we need to do is add $18 + 19 + 20 + 21 + 22$ and to multiply the result by 17.

• Notice that if we subtract 2 from 22 and add that 2 to 18, they would both equal 20. Likewise, if we subtract 1 from 21 and add that 1 to 19, they, too, would both equal 20.

• Thus, the answer to the question must be (C), since $17(18 + 19 + 20 + 21 + 22)$ can be simplified as follows:

$$17(20 + 20 + 20 + 20 + 20) = 17(100) = 1,700$$

(3) Approximation: When to Round – Another great way to avoid difficult arithmetic is to approximate.

• However, it's important to know when you can approximate and when you can't. In general, most problems that contain phrases such as "approximately", "nearest to", and "closest to" can be solved through approximation.

➢ This is especially true if a problem contains **difficult numbers AND a phrase that means "approximately"**!

• When approximating, be sure **to round your numbers as gently as possible**. You want to round just enough to make the arithmetic easy, but not so much as to distort the information significantly.

In a recent school year, college *C* received $467,000 in alumni contributions. Of these contributions, 12 percent were allocated to campus upkeep. Approximately what amount of those contributions was NOT allocated to campus upkeep?

(A) $4,000   (B) $50,000   (C) $352,000   (D) $410,000   (E) $500,000

Answer. D. According to the question, 12% of the allocations were allocated to campus upkeep. Thus, to determine how much of the contributions were NOT allocated to campus upkeep, we simply need to remove 12% from the total contributions. Because the college received $467,000 in contributions, we can say:

$$\$467{,}000 - 12\% \text{ of } \$467{,}000 = \text{Amount NOT for Upkeep}$$

➢ Since the question contains the word "approximately" AND it's difficult to calculate 12% of 467,000, the best way to solve this problem is to round the numbers.

• In general, **if you need to round two numbers, try to round them in the same direction.** Rounding numbers in opposite directions can exaggerate the effects of rounding. Thus, let's round 12% down to 10% and 467,000 down to 460,000.

• Since 10% of 460,000 is 46,000 (remember, to get 10% of a number, slide it's decimal one space to the left), answer choice (D) must be the correct answer: $410,000 is the only answer close to our approximation of $414,000.

$$\$460{,}000 - \$46{,}000 = \$414{,}000$$

➢ But, be careful: **if a problem contains numbers that CAN be easily handled, do NOT round.** Even if it contains a phrase that means "approximately".

• Rounding in such cases will always produce the WRONG answer. Consider the following sample problem:

Which of the following is most nearly equal to the quotient of $\sqrt{10} \div 2$?

(A) $\frac{2}{3}$ **(B)** $\frac{13}{10}$ **(C)** $\frac{3}{2}$ **(D)** $\frac{8}{5}$ **(E)** $\frac{5}{2}$

Answer. D. As we saw in our chapter on Arithmetic, $\sqrt{10}$ equals 3.2, approximately. Thus, because this question contains the phrase "most nearly equal to", we may be tempted to select answer choice (C).

• After all, rounding 3.2 to 3 gives us $3 \div 2$, which is another way of saying 3/2.

➢ Doing so, however, would be a MISTAKE: this problem does not contain difficult numbers. $3.2 \div 2$ is easy to work with. Half of 3.2 is 1.6.

• Since our answer should equal 1.6, approximately, we know that answer choices (A) and (E) are wrong: 2/3 equals $0.\overline{6}$, since $1/3 = 0.\overline{3}$, and $5/2 = 2.5$. Likewise, we know that answer choice (B) is also wrong, since $13/10 = 1.3$.

• 8/5 is another way of saying $8 \div 5$. Remember, to divide a number by 5, you can multiply it by 2 and then divide it by 10. Thus, the correct answer must be (D), since $8 \times 2 = 16$ and $16 \div 10 = 1.6$.

➢ Finally, **beware of the "Rounding Trap"**. Exam-makers know that some test-takers will round.

• From time to time, therefore, they design questions that are intended to confuse test-takers who do.

• Consider the following question:

When walking, a certain person takes 14 complete steps in 10 seconds. At this rate, how many complete steps does this person take in 79 seconds?

(A) 56   **(B)** 82   **(C)** 91   **(D)** 110   **(E)** 130

Answer. D. To start, notice that this question does not contain a word or phrase that means "approximately". However, notice that its answer choices are fairly dispersed.

> ➢ If your problem contains answer choices that are spread apart AND numbers that are difficult to work with, it's SAFE to round.

• **You never want to approximate if the answers are tightly bunched.**

• For example, answer choices such as (A) 56, (B) 58, (C) 59, (D) 60, (E) 62 would be TOO CLOSE together to consider rounding. Answer such as (A) 56, (B) 82, (C) 91, (D) 110, (E) 130, however, have sufficient space between them to consider rounding.

> ➢ To solve this problem, let's round 14 up to 15 and 79 up to 80. If a person takes 15 steps every 10 seconds, then he or she takes 1.5 steps every second.

• And if a person walks at this rate for 80 seconds, then he or she should take 120 steps during that time, since:

$$80 \text{ sec} \times 1.5 \text{ steps/sec} \rightarrow 80(1+0.5) \rightarrow 80+40 = 120 \text{ steps}$$

• Notice that our answer, 120, put us right in the middle of answer choices (D) 110 and (E) 130. **We've fallen right into the "Rounding Trap": our rounding has put us exactly between two answer choices.**

> ➢ To climb out, we simply need to understand HOW our rounding AFFECTED our answer.

• Looking back, notice that we increased the rate of our walker AND increased the length of time that he or she walked.

• In other words, our rounding inflated the number of steps that the walker took. Therefore, our answer must be slightly smaller than our approximated answer of 120, making answer choice (D) the correct answer.

(4) Subtract the Common Elements! – Comparisons are another place where "smart math" can help you avoid difficult arithmetic.

- Comparisons are a big part of GRE math.

  ➢ On every exam, 15 of the 40 math questions are Quantitative Comparison questions. What's more, Problem Solving questions can involve comparisons too.

- When comparing quantities, **you can always SUBTRACT what the quantities have in common** to make the comparison easier.

- To illustrate this concept, let's first consider a straightforward problem:

Quantity A	Quantity B
13(11) + 412	412 + 10(14)

Answer. A. Since Quantities A and B have 412 in common, we can subtract 412 from each quantity to make the comparison easier:

13(11) + ~~412~~	~~412~~ + 10(14)

- Doing so proves that Quantity A must be greater than Quantity B, since 143 is greater than 140:

$$13(11) = 130 + 13 = 143 \qquad 10(14) = 140$$

  ➢ Now, let's consider a more difficult problem:

Quantity A	Quantity B
$2,341 \times 123,456$	$2,342 \times 123,455$

Answer. B. Although we may be tempted to solve this problem by calculator, the numbers are simply too big: using the calculator will result in an "Error" message.

  ➢ We may also be tempted to multiply these numbers by hand.

- But remember: **any question that invites you to do a lot of busy work is likely fishing for something else.**

> ➤ When comparing these quantities, you may notice that their numbers are very similar: 2,342 is 1 bigger than 2,341 and 123,456 is 1 bigger than 123,455.

• In other words, $2,341 \times 123,456$ can be understood as $2,341 \times (123,455 + 1)$. Likewise, $2,342 \times 123,455$ can be understood as $(2,341 + 1) \times 123,455$.

• We can use this observation to rewrite Quantities A and B as follows:

Quantity A	Quantity B
$2,341 \times (123,455 + 1)$	$(2,341 + 1) \times 123,455$

> ➤ As a next step, we can distribute the information within these two quantities, like this:

Quantity A	Quantity B
$2,341 \times (123,455 + 1)$	$(2,341 + 1) \times 123,455$

• If we write out the distribution for each quantity, we can express Quantities A and B as follows:

Quantity A	Quantity B
$\mathbf{2,341 \times 123,455} + 2,341 \times 1$	$\mathbf{2,341 \times 123,455} + 1 \times 123,455$

> ➤ As you can see, the two quantities have a COMMON element: $2,341 \times 123,455$. Thus, we can SUBTRACT this element to make the comparison easier.

• Doing so leaves us with the following, proving that Quantity B is considerably greater than Quantity A:

Quantity A	Quantity B
$2,341 \times 1$	$1 \times 123,455$

• The correct answer is therefore (B).

Using the Answers

---

(5) Backsolving – Our second group of "Plan B" strategies involves using the answer choices.

• The first of these strategies is commonly referred to as backsolving, which is probably the most well-known of all the "Plan B" strategies.

➤ Backsolving is the simple act of **plugging the answer choices back into the question** in order to solve it.

• It can be a strikingly effective technique, particularly for problems **whose answers are simple whole numbers** and where the alternative is to set up or solve complex algebraic equations.

• To understand how backsolving works, consider the following example:

Today is Sarah's 8th birthday and her mother's 36th birthday. How many years from today will Sarah's mother be three times as old as Sarah is at that time?

(A) 4   (B) 6   (C) 8   (D) 9   (E) 10

Answer. B. When encountering such a problem, your first instinct may be to solve it algebraically. And that's fine. In fact, we encourage it: we want you to embrace solving problems the right way. It's the most important key to success on the GRE.

➤ However, if you find the problem confusing, or find yourself presented with a lot of busy work, you might ask yourself whether plugging in the answer choices can help.

• Especially if the answers are SIMPLE numbers.

• Let's try the "plugging" tactic here. Imagine for a moment that (A) were the correct choice. Four years from today, Sarah would be 12 and her mother 40. However, since 40 is not three times as old as 12, (A) cannot be the answer.

➤ Next, imagine that (B) were the correct answer. Six years from today, Sarah would be 14 and her mother 42.

• **Since 42 is three times as old as 14, (B) must be the correct answer.** We could quickly test out the remaining answers, but there's no need to do so: only one of these answers can be correct.

- If you can solve this problem without this technique: great! We still encourage you, however, to incorporate backsolving into your "bag of tricks". Having **the flexibility to solve a problem in multiple ways can only improve your chances for success**.

  ➤ Although backsolving is traditionally thought of as a technique for Problem Solving questions, it can also be used for Quantitative Comparison questions, too.

- Consider the following:

A chair manufacturer has determined that its gross revenue, in terms of x, the number of chairs sold, is given by the expression $x^2 + x - 132$.

Quantity A	Quantity B
The number of chairs that must be sold for the gross revenue to be zero	10

Answer: A. To solve this problem algebraically, we would need to recognize that the expression $x^2 + x - 132$ must be set equal to zero and to factor the resulting quadratic equation: two things you will learn to do in our book on <u>Number Properties & Algebra</u>.

  ➤ However, even if you can already do so, notice that it's FAR easier to backsolve this problem.

- If x were to equal 10, the gross revenue of the company would be LESS THAN ZERO:

$$10^2 + 10 - 132 \quad \rightarrow \quad 100 + 10 - 132 = -22$$

- Since Quantity A represents the number of chairs that must be sold for the gross revenue to equal zero, Quantity A must therefore be larger than 10.

  ➤ But be careful. As effective as backsolving can be, let's not exaggerate its importance.

- For starters, **less than 10% of GRE math problems can be solved with backsolving**. This means that on a typical exam it can help you solve fewer than 4 of the 40 math problems. So, don't let it become a crutch.

- Further, **backsolving can be time-consuming**. Even when it works, there is often a better way to solve the problem. Consider the following:

If 12*x* = 5*y* + 88 and *y* = –2*x*, what is the value of *x*?

(A) 1 (B) 2 (C) 3 (D) 4 (E) 5

Answer. D. Because these answer choices are simple whole numbers, we might consider backsolving to determine the value of *x*.

➢ To start, we could first test (A). If *x* were to equal 1, then *y* would equal –2, since *y* = –2*x*. However, if *x* = 1 and *y* = –2, then the initial equation would be false:

$$12x = 5y + 88$$
$$12(1) \neq 5(-2) + 88$$

• Thus (A) cannot be the correct answer. Likewise, if *x* were to equal 2, then *y* would equal –4, since *y* = –2*x*. However, if *x* = 2 and *y* = –4, then the initial equation would again be false, proving that (B) cannot be correct either:

$$12x = 5y + 88$$
$$12(2) \neq 5(-4) + 88$$

• And we could continue in this vein until we reach the correct answer. However, it's abundantly clear that backsolving is not a great idea for this question. **We might have to repeat these steps four or five times before stumbling upon the correct answer.**

➢ In contrast, if we solve this problem algebraically, we only have to do the work ONCE. Because *y* = –2*x*, we can plug this info into 12*x* = 5*y* + 88 as follows:

$$12x = 5(-2x) + 88$$

• And since 5(–2*x*) = –10*x*, we can lump the like terms together to solve for *x*, proving that (D) is the correct answer:

$$12x = -10x + 88$$
$$22x = 88$$
$$x = 4$$

➢ In summation, we encourage you to embrace backsolving, **particularly when the answer choices are SIMPLE whole numbers.**

• And it never hurts to ask yourself whether plugging the answer choices can help you if you find a problem confusing.

• But remember, it may not be the best approach, even if the answers are whole numbers. **Only use it when you feel it can help you solve a problem quickly, or if you're stuck.**

(6) "Which of the Following" Questions – "Which of the following" questions (WOTF's) are another smart place to use the answer choices.

• WOTF's are easy to spot because (surprise!) they always include the phrase "which of the following".

➤ WOTF's are special because in many cases the only way to solve them is to work through the answer choices.

• **In many cases, the answer to WOTF's is either (A) or (E).**

• This is not accidental. Exam-makers know that test-takers will work through the answer choices in the most logical way possible: first (A), then (B), then (C), and so forth.

➤ As such, exam-makers often make the correct answer choice (E) to induce test-takers to waste as much time as possible.

• Conversely, exam-makers also know that some test-takers understand this, and so make the answer (A) to induce test-takers who work through the answer backwards to waste their time. (Yes, exam-makers are a devious sort!)

➤ When solving WOTF's, **be sure to try answer choice (A) first. If that doesn't work, then try (E).** In many (but not all) cases, it will be one of the two.

• If neither works, try (D), then (C), then (B). Consider the following question:

Which of the following is equal to 24,500,000?

(A) $(24 \times 10^7) + (5 \times 10^6)$
(B) $(2.4 \times 10^{-7}) + (5 \times 10^{-5})$
(C) $(2 \times 10^6) + (4 \times 10^5) + (5 \times 10^4)$
(D) $(2 \times 10^{-7}) + (4 \times 10^{-6}) + (5 \times 10^{-5})$
(E) $(2 \times 10^7) + (4 \times 10^6) + (5 \times 10^5)$

Answer. E. This question is a WOTF, since it contains the phrase "which of the following". To solve WOTF's, it's usually necessary (or easiest) to work through the answer choices.

• Since the correct answer to many WOTF's is either (A) or (E), we should first try answer choice (A). If that doesn't work, we should try (E) next.

➢ As you will learn in our discussion of Decimals, multiplying a number by 10^n will slide its decimal n spaces to the right.

• For example, $5.71 \times 10^3 = 5,710$, since 10^3 slides the decimal of 5.71 three spaces to the right.

• As such, answer choice (A) cannot be correct: $24 \times 10^7 = 240,000,000$, since 10^7 slides the decimal place of 24 seven spaces to the right.

➢ Let's next look at answer choice (E). If multiplying a number by 10^n slides its decimal n spaces to the right, then:

$$2 \times 10^7 = 20,000,000 \qquad 4 \times 10^6 = 4,000,000 \qquad 5 \times 10^5 = 500,000$$

• Thus, answer choice (E) must be correct, since:

$$
\begin{array}{r}
20,000,000 \\
4,000,000 \\
+ \quad 500,000 \\
\hline
24,500,000
\end{array}
$$

(7) Check the Answers for Clues! – Keeping an eye on the answer choices is yet another way to save time.

- **The answer choices are additional pieces of information**. If we ignore them, we ignore potential clues.

  ➤ Remember, exam-makers often bait test-takers into doing more work than is necessary.

- If your question invites you to do a lot of busy work, **it's always worth your while to check out the answer choices**. From time to time, they may offer information that will save you from that busy work.

- Consider the following question:

$$(2 \times 100) + (4 \times 1,000) + (5 \times 10) + (7 \times 10,000) + (3 \times 1) =$$

(A) 72,345   (B) 27,354   (C) 43,527   (D) 34,275   (E) 74,253

Answer. E. Although we can solve this problem by multiplying each term in the question and adding their sums, we can easily skip this work. Notice that our number should end in a 3, since the term **3 × 1 will produce its last digit.**

- Since (E) is the only answer choice that ends in a 3, the answer must be 74,253.

  ➤ In some cases, the answer choices may not help you until you're half way through a problem.

- It's always worth your while to keep an eye on the answer choices, no matter how deep into the problem you may be.

- Consider the following question:

The population of a certain town was 10,000 exactly three decades ago. The size of the population increased by 10 percent during the first decade, increased by 5 percent during the second decade, and decreased by 10 percent during the third decade. What is the population of the town today?

(A) 10,350   (B) 10,395   (C) 10,500   (D) 11,500   (E) 12,705

Answer. B. Using the 10% shortcut, we know that the population of the town must have been 11,000 after the first decade, since 10% of 10,000 = 1,000.

- We also know that the population of the town must have been 11,550 after the second decade, since 10% of 11,000 = 1,100, and half of that is 550.

  ➤ To determine the population of the town after the third decade, we need to subtract 10% of 11,550 from 11,550.

- Remember, to take 10% of a number, simply slide its decimal point one place to the left. Thus, 10% of 11,550 = 1,155.

- Finally to subtract 1,155 from 11,550, we can line up the two numbers as follows:

$$
\begin{array}{r}
11{,}550 \\
-\quad 1{,}155 \\
\hline
\ldots 5
\end{array}
$$

  ➤ Rather than complete this subtraction, however, **notice that the difference MUST END in a 5**.

- Of the given answer choices, only two of them end in a 5: (B) and (E). And only one of these is less than 11,550. Hence, (B) must be the correct answer.

Picking Numbers

(8) Picking Numbers – As the title suggests, our third group of "Plan B" strategies involves picking numbers.

• Picking numbers is a great way of turning confusing, abstract problems into simple, less intimidating ones.

> ➤ The strategy works by **replacing unknowns with numbers that are easy to handle**, and then solving the problem using those numbers.

• Since it's easier to work with numbers than variables or abstract relationships, picking numbers can be dramatically simpler (and faster) than more algebraic approaches.

• There are a variety of situations in which you can pick numbers to solve a problem, but, in general, all of these situations share one feature: **the problem contains no CONCRETE values**.

> ➤ For example, a problem in which "John eats 1/3 of a pizza and his friends eat 60% of what remains" would be a great candidate for picking numbers.

• There is no information about how much the pizza weighs or how many slices it has. Values such as "1/3" and "60%" are RELATIVE. 1/3 of this pizza could equal 2 slices, 5 slices, or 10 pounds. **Without a concrete value, we simply don't how large the pizza is**.

• A problem in which "John eats 1/3 of a pizza and his friends eat 60% of the remaining 10 slices", however, would NOT be a good candidate for picking numbers. After all, if John eats 1/3 of a pizza and 10 slices remain, **we know exactly how large the pizza is**, since the 10 slices left over must equal the remaining 2/3 of the pizza.

> ➤ When picking numbers, it doesn't matter whether your problem involves Rates, Geometry, Formulas, or Number Properties.

• As long as your problem LACKS concrete values, you can ALWAYS pick numbers to solve it.

• Just **be sure to pick numbers that are EASY to work with**. Choosing large or awkward numbers (e.g. 2,000 or 19) will only make the work harder. Remember, the goal of this strategy is to simplify problems, not complicate them!

➤ Likewise, if you need to pick TWO numbers, choose **numbers that work well together**.

• For example, if your first choice is 3, your next choice might be 12 or 30, since 12 and 30 are divisible by 3. Consider the following:

The quantities A and B are positive and are related by the equation $A = \frac{x}{B}$, where x is a constant. If the value of B increases by 25 percent, then the value of A decreases by what percent?

(A) 20%   (B) $33\frac{1}{3}$%   (C) 40%   (D) 50%   (E) $66\frac{2}{3}$%

Answer. A. Since **this problem contains no concrete values**, we can solve it by picking numbers. The value of B is said to increase by 25%.

➤ A good choice for B would be 4, since 25% of 4 = 1. And if $B = 4$, a good choice for x would be 40, since 4 and 40 work well together.

• If $B = 4$ and $x = 40$, then A initially equals 10, since:

$$A = \frac{x}{B} \;\rightarrow\; A = \frac{40}{4} = 10$$

• If B increases by 25%, then B equals 5, since 25% of 4 = 1. And if x is a constant, i.e. a value that doesn't change, then x still equals 40. Thus, if $B = 5$ and $x = 40$, then A decreases to 8, since:

$$A = \frac{x}{B} \;\rightarrow\; A = \frac{40}{5} = 8$$

➤ To determine a percent change: **place the difference between the new and original values over the original value**, and then multiply the result by 100.

• If the value of A decreases from 10 to 8, then the correct answer must be (A), since a change from 10 to 8 represents a 20 percent decrease in value:

$$\frac{\text{Difference}}{\text{Original}} \times 100 = \frac{2}{10} \times 100 = 20\%$$

➤ When picking numbers, it's important that you respect any CONSTRAINTS within the problem.

• If your unknown is supposed to be divisible by 2, and you pick a value such as 5, you're violating the parameters of the question. It's also important to remember that ZERO and TWO are special: zero is neither positive nor negative, and two is the only even prime.

➤ On a final note: when picking numbers for problems involving MULTIPLES, FACTORS, or REMAINDERS, **we encourage you to pick several numbers**.

• If you only pick one number in such problems, you may mislead yourself. Let's take a look at another problem:

If a certain integer x is a multiple of both 7 and 9, which of the following must be true?

Select all such statements.

A x is an odd integer.   **B** x is equal to 63.   **C** x is a multiple of 21.

Answer: C only. Because this problem has no concrete values, we can pick numbers to solve it. However, we can't pick just any value for x.

➤ **Whatever we pick has to obey the constraints of the problem**: x has to be a multiple of 7 and 9.

• A multiple of 7 is a number divisible by 7, and a multiple of 9 is a number divisible by 9. One number that is clearly divisible by both 7 and 9 is 63, the product of 7×9.

• As such, you might be tempted to select $\boxed{A}$, $\boxed{B}$, and $\boxed{C}$ as the correct answer. (In the case of $\boxed{C}$, 63 would be considered a multiple of 21, since 63 is divisible by 21: $63 \div 21 = 3$.) However, 63 isn't the only number divisible by 7 and 9.

➤ When picking numbers for problems involving multiples, factors, or remainders, we encourage you to ask yourself **"is there only one number that I can pick?"**

• Remember, there may be several numbers that satisfy the constraints of your problem. If so, try to pick 2 or 3 examples. **If you pick just one, you may mislead yourself.**

• Another number divisible by 7 and 9 **is the number twice as big** as 63: 126. To prove it, we can chunk 126 into $70 + 56$. Each of these chunks is divisible by 7, so 126 is divisible by 7. Likewise, 126 is divisible by 9, since the sum of its digits is divisible by 9: $1 + 2 + 6 = 9$.

➤ Since x can also equal 126, our answer cannot be $\boxed{A}$ or $\boxed{B}$: x doesn't have to be odd or equal 63.

• Further, "Select One or More Questions" (like the one above) must have at least one correct answer, so $\boxed{C}$ must be true. If $\boxed{C}$ were false, we would have no correct answers.

(9) PUQ's and FUQ's – There are two types of problems without concrete values that are frequently encountered on the GRE.

- We call them PUQ's and FUQ's.

  ➢ The term "PUQ" is an acronym that stands for "**Percent** problems with **Unspecified Quantities** (or values)".

- As with any problem without concrete values, the key to solving PUQ's is to pick numbers. Replacing unknown quantities with real numbers dramatically increases the ease of solving such problems.

  ➢ If a percent problem does not include a specified amount, **let the original value equal 100**.

- Picking 100 will make the math simpler for you. Consider the following:

The population of country X increased by 20 percent from 1984 to 1991 and decreased by 10 percent from 1991 to 1998. By what percent did the population of country X increase from 1984 to 1998?

(A) 5% (B) 8% (C) 10% (D) 12% (E) 30%

Answer. B. Since the exact population of country X is **unspecified**, let's pretend that the population of country X in 1984 equals 100. (There's nothing saying that it CAN'T be 100, so we may as well make things easier for ourselves.)

  ➢ A 20% **increase** in the size of the population would raise it from 100 to 120, since 20% of 100 = 20.

- Likewise, a subsequent decrease of 10% would then lower the population from 120 to 108, since 10% of 120 = 12.

- As you will learn when we cover percents, to determine a percent change: place **the difference between the new and original values over the original value**, and then multiply the result by 100.

  ➢ Thus, the percent change in the population of country X from 1984 to 1998 was 8%, since:

$$\frac{\text{Difference}}{\text{Original}} = \frac{108-100}{100} \times 100 = \frac{8}{100} \times 100 = 8\%$$

- The correct answer is therefore (B).

- FUQ's are very similar to PUQ's.

  ➢ The term "FUQ" is also an acronym. It stands for "**Fraction** problems with **Unspecified Quantities** (or values)".

- As with PUQ's, the key to solving FUQ's is to pick numbers.

- If a fraction problem does not include a specified amount, **pick a number equal to the PRODUCT of EVERY denominator** involved.

  ➢ Doing so will make the math dramatically easier for you. Consider the following:

Jake ate $\frac{1}{3}$ of a cake, Emily ate $\frac{1}{5}$ of the remaining cake, and Zeke ate what was left.

Quantity A	**Quantity B**
The fraction of the cake that Zeke ate	$\frac{8}{15}$

Answer: C. This problem contains fractional quantities, but no actual values. Thus, we can pick numbers.

- Since this problem contains the fractions 1/3 and 1/5, and the product of 3 × 5 = 15, let's pretend that the cake consists of 15 identical slices.

  ➢ If Jack eats 1/3 of those 15 slices, then Jack eats 5 slices and leaves 10, since 1/3 of 15 = 5.

- Likewise, if Emily eats 1/5 of the slices **that Jack leaves**, then Emily eats 2 slices and leaves 8, since 1/5 of the 10 left by Jack = 2.

- Thus, if Zeke eats **what Jake and Emily do not**, Zeke must eat the remaining 8 slices. Because Zeke eats 8 of the 15 slices, the correct answer is therefore (C).

> ➢ But, be careful. **If your problem contains even ONE real value, you CANNOT pick numbers**.

• Such problems are NOT PUQ's or FUQ's and must always be solved algebraically. Consider the following:

The price of a certain couch was recently reduced by 30 percent. If that couch is now $45 less expensive, what was the original price of the couch?

(A) $100   (B) $115   (C) $125   (D) $135   (E) $150

Answer: E. Although this problem may seem like a PUQ, it is not: it contains the real value $45. Thus, **we cannot let the original value of the couch equal $100**.

> ➢ We can, however, recognize that "30% of the original price" = $45. This relationship can be used to determine 100% of the original price by means of the following proportion:

$$\frac{30 \text{ percent}}{45 \text{ dollars}} = \frac{100 \text{ percent}}{x \text{ dollars}}$$

• Cross-multiplication reveals that the original price of the couch was $150, since:

$$30x = 45(100) \quad \rightarrow \quad x = \frac{45(10\cancel{0})}{3\cancel{0}} = \frac{45(10)}{3} = \frac{\cancel{3}(15)(10)}{\cancel{3}} = \$150$$

• Thus, the correct answer is (E). As always, **don't worry if the math here confuses you**. All of these concepts will be covered properly in due time.

> ➢ For the time being, our only hope is that you understand one thing: you can pick numbers when your problem lacks concrete values.

• If that problem contains PERCENTS, pick **100**. If that problem contains FRACTIONS, pick the **product** of **every denominator**.

• And if you're still unclear on what we mean by PUQ's and FUQ's, never fear: we will revisit these strategies later on. You will find a discussion of PUQ's in the Percents chapter of our book on <u>Word Problems</u> and a discussion of FUQ's in the Fractions chapter of this book.

(10) "Asswholes" – Problems that contain **variables in their answer choices** can be among the most difficult problems encountered on the GRE.

- That is, unless you know the "asswhole" strategy.

  ➢ We call it the "asswhole" strategy because **the strategy is to "ass"ign "whole" numbers** to variables within the question.

- In general, problems that contain variables in their answer choices can be solved algebraically or by assigning numbers.

- Assigning numbers is almost always the smarter strategy. In many cases, dramatically so: **some "asswholes" are very difficult to solve without assigning numbers**.

  ➢ The strategy is a two-step process:

- FIRST, **replace all variables in the problem by picking numbers**, then solve the problem using those numbers.

- SECOND, once you've solved the problem, **plug the values you've picked for the variables into the answer choices** to see which answer matches your solution.

  ➢ As always, pick numbers that are easy to work with. **The prime numbers 2, 3, 5, and 7 are particularly good choices for "asswholes"**, in many cases.

- Likewise, if you need to pick two or more numbers, pick numbers that work well together. To get a sense of how this technique works, consider the following:

The sum of the ages of Bailey and Celine is x years. If Celine is 8 years older than Bailey, how many years old will Celine be x years from now, in terms of x?

(A) $x-4$ (B) $2x+4$ (C) $\frac{x}{2}-4$ (D) $\frac{3x}{2}+4$ (E) $\frac{5x}{2}-4$

Answer. D. Because this problem has **variables in its answer choices**, we can solve it algebraically or we can use the "asswhole" strategy.

- For the sake of practice, let's use the "asswhole" approach. To start, let's pick a value for x. Any value will do, but it's always best to work with small, simple numbers. Let's also be sure to **respect the constraints within the problem**.

- According to the problem, x is "the sum of the ages of Bailey and Celine", and Celine is "8 years older than Bailey," so **any value that we pick for x needs to be greater than 8**.

  ➢ If Bailey were 2, then Celine would be 10, and their combined ages would be 12. So let's make $x = 12$.

- Finally, the problem asks "how many years old will Celine be x years from now?" According to the numbers we've chosen, Celine is currently 10 and $x = 12$.

- Therefore, Celine should be 22 years old x years from now, since $10 + 12 = 22$.

  ➢ Thus, to solve this problem, we only have to **plug $x = 12$ into the answer choices to see which answer matches our solution**: $\boxed{22}$.

- Doing so proves that (D) is the correct answer, since (D) is the only choice that equals 22:

(A) $x - 4 \quad \rightarrow \quad 12 - 4 = \boxed{8}$

(B) $2x + 4 \quad \rightarrow \quad 2(12) + 4 = \boxed{28}$

(C) $\frac{x}{2} - 4 \quad \rightarrow \quad \frac{12}{2} - 4 = \boxed{2}$

(D) $\frac{3x}{2} + 4 \quad \rightarrow \quad \frac{3(12)}{2} + 4 = 3(6) + 4 = \boxed{22}$

(E) $\frac{5x}{2} - 4 \quad \rightarrow \quad \frac{5(12)}{2} - 4 = 5(6) - 4 = \boxed{26}$

  ➢ If you can solve this problem without this technique: great! We still encourage you, however, to incorporate the strategy into your "bag of tricks".

- There are plenty of "asswholes" more difficult than this (some dramatically so), and the flexibility to solve a problem in multiple ways can only improve your chances for success.

  ➢ When picking numbers, it's important that you **obey the following rules**.

- Exam-makers are aware that some test-takers pick numbers. Consequently, they design answer choices every now and then that foil commonly chosen numbers.

- As long as you obey these rules, you will avoid the traps that exam-makers set for you:

  1. **Do not pick the same number more than once.**
  2. **Avoid numbers you see in the question or in the answer choices.**
  3. **Stay away from 0, 1, and 100.**

• In other words, **if you have to choose values for two variables, don't pick the same number for both.** And if you see the number 5 in the question, or the number 10 is the answer choices, don't pick 5 or 10.

> ➤ Finally, one last bit of advice: when you plug your numbers into the answer choices, try (A) first. If (A) doesn't work, try (E) next.

• As with "Which of the Following Questions", **the correct answer to "asswhole" problems is frequently (A) or (E).** Trying (A) and then (E) may save you time. Let's take a look at a second example:

Lydia bought a book of 200 identical stamps at a total cost of p dollars. If Lydia then sold each stamp at a rate that was 40 percent above the original, then, in terms of p, for how many dollars was each stamp sold?

$$\text{(A) } \frac{7p}{1,000} \quad \text{(B) } \frac{7p}{20} \quad \text{(C) } 140p \quad \text{(D) } \frac{p}{200} + 40 \quad \text{(E) } \frac{140}{p} \cdot 100$$

Answer. A. To start, let's make $p = 400$. This number is unique, **since it is not found in the question or the answer choices.** It also produces simple, positive whole numbers when combined with the "200" in the problem.

> ➤ Hence, if Lydia bought 200 stamps for $400, she originally paid $2 per stamp, as $400/200 stamps = $2/stamp.

• And if Lydia sold each stamp at a rate that is 40% **above the original**, she sold each stamp for $2.80 : 10% of $2.00 = $0.20, so 40% = 4 × $0.20 = $0.80.

• Plugging $p = 400$ into the answer choices reveals that (A) is the correct answer, since (A) is the only answer choice that equals $2.80:

(A) $\dfrac{7p}{1,000}$ → $\dfrac{7(400)}{1,000} = \boxed{2.8}$

(E) $\dfrac{140}{p} \cdot 100$ → $\dfrac{140}{400} \cdot 100 = \boxed{35}$

(D) $\dfrac{p}{200} + 40$ → $\dfrac{400}{200} + 40 = \boxed{42}$

(C) $140p$ → $140(400) = \boxed{56,000}$

(B) $\dfrac{7p}{20}$ → $\dfrac{7(400)}{20} = \boxed{140}$

> As with **"Which of the Following" Questions**, if (A) and (E) DON'T work, try (D), then (C), then (B).

(11) The Hybrid Approach – The downside of the "asswhole" strategy is that it can be time-consuming, particularly if the answer choices contain **multiple variables**.

• Because each variable needs to be plugged in, and then the entire answer calculated, it's easy to spend a lot of time solving the answer choices.

➤ The hybrid approach is a godsend for problems with **multiple variables in the answer choices**.

• Like the "asswhole" strategy, the hybrid approach encourages you to pick numbers to solve problems with variables in the answer choices. Unlike the "asswhole" strategy, however, **it does not require you to plug those numbers back into the answer choices**.

• In a sense, the hybrid approach is the best of both worlds: it incorporates the simplicity of picking numbers but does away with the need to compute the answer choices.

➤ The approach is a two-step process:

• FIRST, **replace all variables in the problem by picking numbers**, then solve the problem using those numbers.

• SECOND, use that solution to **tease out the mathematical relationship** among the variables in the question.

➤ For example, imagine your question contains the variables a, b, and c, for which you choose the values $a = 4$, $b = 5$, and $c = 10$.

• Then, imagine the solution to your problem is 8.

• If that 8 was the result of $4(10) \div 5$, then your answer would have to equal $ac \div b$, since the $4 = a$, $10 = c$, and $5 = b$. Similarly, if that 8 was the result of $4^2(5) \div 10$, then your answer would have to equal $a^2 b \div c$.

➤ To get a proper sense of how this technique works, let's work through a problem together.

• Consider the following:

If a certain student scores an average (arithmetic mean) of r points per quiz for q quizzes and then scores a total of p points on her next quiz, what is the student's average score for the $q + 1$ quizzes?

(A) $\dfrac{qr+p}{q+1}$ (B) $r+\dfrac{p}{q+1}$ (C) $p+\dfrac{r}{q+1}$ (D) $\dfrac{q(r+p)}{q+1}$ (E) $\dfrac{r+pq}{q+1}$

Answer. A. If we let $r = 5$ and $q = 4$, then the student scores a total of 20 points on her first 4 quizzes. Further, if we let $p = 10$, then she scores a total of 30 points for all 5 quizzes, giving her an average score of 6.

➤ If we plug $r = 5$, $q = 4$, and $p = 10$ into answer choice (A), we see that (A) is the correct answer, since:

$$\text{(A)} \quad \frac{qr+p}{q+1} = \frac{4(5)+10}{4+1} = \frac{20+10}{5} = \frac{30}{5} = 6$$

• Note, however, that it would take a long time to plug all three values into all five of our answer choices: especially if the correct answer were not (A) or (E).

➤ **We can solve problems like this more quickly by asking ourselves: "how did we get an average score of 6?"**

• Here, we know that the 6 came from $30 \div 5$. We also know that the 30 came from $20 + 10$ and that the 5 came from $4 + 1$.

➤ Since the $20 = 4(5) = qr$, and the $10 = p$, the numerator of the answer must be $qr + p$. Likewise, since the $4 + 1 = q + 1$, the denominator of the answer must be $q + 1$.

• Thus, the correct answer is (A):

$$\frac{30}{5} = \frac{20+10}{5} = \frac{4(5)+10}{4+1} = \frac{qr+p}{q+1}$$

➤ Ultimately, the hybrid approach offers a great blend of simplicity and speed. From time to time, however, it **can be difficult to execute**, particularly with advanced problems.

• If you can't make the algebra work, be prepared to fall back on the "asswhole" strategy. Even in the few instances when the technique is slower than classical algebra, it will at least get you the correct answer.

Guess Strategies

(12) Split the Answers – Our final group of "Plan B" strategies is a small collection of tips and techniques for guessing.

• In general, this group is considerably less useful than the first three, since its strategies are mostly "elimination strategies".

> ➤ In other words, they're not intended to help you solve problems. They're intended to help you **get rid of bad answers**.

• So, use one or more of them if you're low on time, or know of no other way to attack your problem.

• But **don't spend too much time on any of these**. Make a quick, educated guess and save your time for problems where it's better spent!

> ➤ The first can be used for Problem Solving questions and relies on something that many test-takers never notice: **the answer choices are given in ORDER**.

• In general, **this order is from least to greatest**, though in some cases the order may be from greatest to least.

• This observation may seem trivial, but it often proves helpful when it comes to guessing. It allows us to "**split the answers**" into a big group and a little group.

> ➤ In many problems, it's often easy to eliminate an answer because it's clearly too big or too small.

• Imagine, for example, that answer choice (C) is too big. If the answer choices are given from least to greatest, then (D) and (E) must also be too big.

• You might think, "wouldn't it be obvious that (D) and (E) are bigger?" Sometimes. But there are plenty of situations where the values of the answer choices are less clear, particularly if they contain **roots, fractions, or π**.

- Consider the following:

$$\sqrt{9(16) + 18(2)} \text{ is equal to which of the following?}$$

(A) 8   (B) $6\sqrt{5}$ (C) 14   (D) $8\sqrt{5}$ (E) $14\sqrt{5}$

Answer. B. Perhaps you know how to find the value of this square root. If so, great! If not, no worries: you will learn how to do so in the Roots chapter of this book. For the time being, let's imagine that you don't.

> ➤ Like many test-takers, your first instinct might be to multiply the terms inside the root. Technically, this is not the best way to break down this root.

- However, doing so would leave you with the square root of 180:

$$\sqrt{9(16) + 18(2)} = \sqrt{144 + 36} = \sqrt{180}$$

- Even if we can't work the problem further, we still have enough information to determine that (B) must be the correct answer.

> ➤ The GRE lists answer choices in order. From answer choices (A) and (C), it's clear that **the choices are arranged in order from least to greatest.**

- From answer choice (C), it's also clear that **our answer has to be (A) or (B):** $14 = \sqrt{196}$ (memorize those squares!) and $\sqrt{180} < \sqrt{196}$, so our answer has to be smaller than (C).

- Finally, we can rule out answer choice (A) since it's obviously too small: $8 = \sqrt{64}$. Thus, (B) is the only answer that can be correct.

> ➤ Of course, "splitting the answers" is not always this effective.

- It can, however, be a quick, simple way of **exposing answer choices that are too big** or too little to be correct.

- And though narrowing down the answers to a final two or three will never feel great, statistically it's likely to pay off: especially if you have to do so more than once.

<u>**(13) Pick a Test Number**</u> – Another good way to eliminate bad answers is to pick a test number.

- This strategy is a bit like backsolving.

  ➤ As you may recall, backsolving is the act of plugging the answer choices back into the question in order to solve it.

- And it can be very effective with certain problems, particularly problems whose **answers are simple whole numbers**.

- Picking a test number is a great strategy for problems whose **answers are awkward and therefore difficult to plug in**.

  ➤ Because the answers are difficult to use, it can be hard to backsolve such problems, at least in a timely manner.

- There is, however, an easy way around this: **pick a simple number that allows you to "split the answers"**, i.e. cut the answer choices into a group bigger than the number you choose and a group smaller than that number.

- By splitting the answers, your test number should help you determine that some answers are either too big or too small.

  ➤ **The number you pick shouldn't be one of the answer choices**: you don't want to work with awkward numbers that are difficult to compute.

- As with "splitting the answers", this strategy is mostly an "elimination strategy". It may not help you solve your problem, but it will help you **get rid of bad answers**.

- So, use it if you're low on time or know no other way to attack your problem. But **don't spend too much with it**. Make a quick, educated guess and save your time for problems where it's better spent.

  ➤ Let's take a look at a sample question where "picking a test number" can come in handy.

- Consider the following:

Chlorinated water is pumped into an empty 36-gallon filtration tank through pipe A and pumped out of the tank through pipe B. If the rate of flow through A is 2 gallons per hour, how many gallons per hour must flow out of B so that the tank is full in exactly 48 hours?

(A) $\frac{4}{9}$ (B) $\frac{2}{3}$ (C) $\frac{3}{4}$ (D) $\frac{5}{4}$ (E) $\frac{9}{4}$

Answer. D. In the Rates chapter of our book on <u>Word Problems</u>, you will learn how to solve problems like this. For the time being, however, let's pretend that you have no idea how to solve this problem.

➢ One strategy you might consider is backsolving. However, **the answers are not simple whole numbers**, so they're difficult to plug in.

• As such, you might consider picking a test number instead.

• Remember, when picking a test number, **choose a simple whole number that "splits the answers"** into a group bigger than the number you choose and a group smaller than that number. Here, a great choice would be 1, since it's bigger than 3/4 but less than 5/4.

➢ Going back to the problem, we know that 2 gallons per hour flow into the tank.

• **If 1 gallon per hour were to flow out of the tank**, the tank would fill at a net rate of 1 gallon per hour. At this rate, the empty 36-gallon tank would fill in exactly 36 hours.

• But this is too fast: we want the tank to fill in 48 hours. In other words, we need pipe B to pump out more than 1 gallon per hour, in order for the tank to fill more slowly.

➢ **As such, our answer must be larger than 1**. Since only answer choices (D) and (E) are greater than 1, we know that one of these must be the correct answer.

• But we can easily rule out (E) as well. 9/4 is a value greater than 2. After all, 8/4 = 2, and 9/4 > 8/4, so 9/4 must be greater than 2. And if 2 gallons per hour were to flow into the tank and more than 2 gallons per hour were to flow out of the tank, **the tank would never fill!**

• Thus, (D) must be the correct answer, since it's the only answer choice that can possibly solve the problem.

(14) The Quantitative Comparison Guess Trick – This last tip is the least useful of our guess strategies.

• For starters, it's not nearly as safe as splitting the answers or picking a test number. It's purely **an observation of exam-maker tendencies**.

➢ Further, it can only be used in limited situations. Of the 15 quantitative comparison questions on your exam, it may only help you on one of those questions.

• So why teach it at all? Because **the opportunity to use it generally surfaces with very hard questions**.

• And if it can help you correctly answer a hard question that you would otherwise miss, it's worthwhile. It's also very easy to learn:

➢ If one quantity of your comparison is **mathematically complex**, and the other quantity is a **simple number**, the two quantities are OFTEN equal.

• Consider the following:

Set S consists of all the fractions of the form $\frac{n+1}{n}$, where n is a positive integer less than 10.

Quantity A	Quantity B
The product of every fraction in set S	10

Answer: C. Before we solve this the right way, let's note that Quantity A is mathematically complex.

• To obtain its value, we would first need to determine the value of every fraction of the form $\frac{n+1}{n}$, where n is a positive whole number less than 10, and then multiply those fractions together.

➢ In contrast, Quantity B is simply the number 10.

• If we couldn't determine the value of Quantity A, answer choice (C) would be a great guess: in Quantitative Comparison questions where one quantity is a simple number and the other is mathematically complex, **exam-makers have displayed a tendency to make the two quantities equal.**

- To solve this problem correctly, let's first consider what the set of fractions in set S actually looks like.

  ➤ According to the problem, these fractions are in the form $\frac{n+1}{n}$, where n is a positive integer less than 10.

- The term integer means "whole number" and every number greater than zero is positive, so **n can equal all the whole numbers from 1 to 9**.

- In other words, if $n = 1$, a fraction of the form $\frac{n+1}{n}$ would equal $\frac{2}{1}$. Likewise, if $n = 2$, then a fraction of the form $\frac{n+1}{n}$ would equal $\frac{3}{2}$.

  ➤ And if n were to be as large as 9, then a fraction of the form $\frac{n+1}{n}$ would equal $\frac{10}{9}$.

- Thus, if we were to list out all the fractions of this form (where $n = 1, 2, 3, \ldots 8, 9$), and were to multiply them together, we would have the following:

$$\frac{2}{1} \cdot \frac{3}{2} \cdot \frac{4}{3} \cdot \frac{5}{4} \cdot \frac{6}{5} \cdot \frac{7}{6} \cdot \frac{8}{7} \cdot \frac{9}{8} \cdot \frac{10}{9}$$

- Finally, if we were to **cancel out the common terms** before multiplying, we would be left with a 10 on top and a 1 on the bottom, thereby proving that the two quantities are equal:

$$\frac{\cancel{2}}{1} \cdot \frac{\cancel{3}}{\cancel{2}} \cdot \frac{\cancel{4}}{\cancel{3}} \cdot \frac{\cancel{5}}{\cancel{4}} \cdot \frac{\cancel{6}}{\cancel{5}} \cdot \frac{\cancel{7}}{\cancel{6}} \cdot \frac{\cancel{8}}{\cancel{7}} \cdot \frac{\cancel{9}}{\cancel{8}} \cdot \frac{10}{\cancel{9}} = \frac{10}{1} = 10$$

  ➤ Be sure to **use this strategy cautiously**. Unlike "splitting the answers" and picking a test number, this is truly a "desperation strategy": it has no mathematical foundation.

- So, make sure it's the "last option" — only consider it after you've tried everything else.

- And remember, **you should only use it if ONE of your two quantities is truly COMPLEX and the OTHER is a SIMPLE number.** If one of the two quantities is just "sort of hard" or "somewhat simple", it's not likely to pay off for you.

Practice Questions

(15) Problem Sets – We'd like you to solve each of the following questions with one or more of our "Plan B" strategies.

• You may be able to answer some (or many) of these questions without them. If so, great! We still encourage you, however, to incorporate the strategies into your "bag of tricks".

➤ The flexibility to solve a problem in multiple ways can only improve your chances for success.

• Remember: the **most mathematical solution is not always the fastest solution**. Embracing these strategies can save you valuable minutes over the course of your exam.

• For the problems under the header "Part I", use either our "asswhole" strategy or our "hybrid" strategy to attain the correct answer.

➤ For the problems under the header "Part II", use any strategy discussed in this chapter to answer the question.

• If you can't find a solution, use a guess strategy to eliminate as many wrong answers as possible!

Part I

1. A phone call costs $1.00 for the first 5 minutes and $0.40 for each additional minute. If n is an integer greater than 5, a phone call n minutes long will cost how many dollars?

$$\text{(A) } \frac{4n}{5} \quad \text{(B) } \frac{n}{5} - 2 \quad \text{(C) } \frac{n+3}{10} \quad \text{(D) } \frac{2n}{5} - 1 \quad \text{(E) } \frac{3n}{10} + 2$$

2. This year City C has allotted 40 percent of its tax revenue for police and fire services, and its tax revenue is 25 percent higher than last year's tax revenue of d dollars. In terms of d, how many dollars of this year's tax revenue has the city allotted for police and fire services?

$$\text{(A) } 0.4(0.75d) \quad \text{(B) } 0.4(1.25d) \quad \text{(C) } \frac{0.4d}{1.25} \quad \text{(D) } \frac{0.75d}{0.4} \quad \text{(E) } \frac{d}{1.25} + 0.4d$$

3. When integer P is divided by X, the quotient is R and the remainder is T. Which of the following expressions is equal to P?

    (A) RX (B) $R + T$ (C) $RX + T$ (D) $X(R + T)$ (E) $X(R - T)$

4. A certain car travels at a constant rate. If the car travels a miles in b hours, in how many hours will the car travel c miles?

    (A) $\frac{ac}{b}$ (B) $\frac{ab}{c}$ (C) $\frac{bc}{a}$ (D) $\frac{a}{bc}$ (E) $\frac{a+c}{b}$

5. A meal costs x dollars and p percent of those dollars are left as a tip. How much, in dollars, has been paid for the meal, including tip?

    (A) $x(1 + 100p)$ (B) $x(1 + 10p)$ (C) $x(1 + p)$
    (D) $x(1 + 0.1p)$ (E) $x(1 + 0.01p)$

6. $(2xy)^2 + (x^2 - y^2)^2 =$

    (A) $2xy$ (B) $x^2 - y^2$ (C) $x^2 + y^2$ (D) $(2xy)^2 + (x^2 + y^2)^2$ (E) $(x^2 + y^2)^2$

7. A homeless shelter has x boxes of food, each containing 16 identical cans. After distributing c cans to each of a number of recipients, the shelter has p cans left over. Which of the following represents the number of recipients?

    (A) $\frac{16x - p}{c}$ (B) $\frac{16x + p}{c}$ (C) $\frac{16x}{c} - p$ (D) $\frac{16c - p}{x}$ (E) $\frac{16c + p}{x}$

8. A fabric distributor purchased n yards of nylon for x dollars per yard. If p yards of the nylon were lost due to theft and the distributor sold the rest for q dollars per yard, which of the following represents the gross profit on the sale of the nylon?

    (A) $(n - p)q - nx$ (B) $(n - p)x - pq$ (C) $(q - x)p - nx$
    (D) $nx - pq$ (E) $(n - p)(q - x)$

9. A rope of length L inches is cut into two pieces such that the length of one piece is 3 inches more than four times the length of the other piece. Which of the following is the length, in inches, of the longer piece?

    (A) $\frac{5L - 4}{3}$ (B) $\frac{L + 5}{3}$ (C) $\frac{L - 3}{5}$ (D) $\frac{4L + 1}{3}$ (E) $\frac{4L + 3}{5}$

Part II

10. If $n = \sqrt{36 + 36}$, then n equals

   (A) $6\sqrt{2}$ (B) 9   (C) $9\sqrt{2}$ (D) 12   (E) $12\sqrt{2}$

	Quantity A	Quantity B
11.	$17(33) + 33(87)$	3,300

12. When 15 is divided by the positive integer n, the remainder is $n - 3$. Which of the following could be the value of n?

   (A) 4   (B) 5   (C) 6   (D) 7   (E) 8

13. If p is a prime number between 3 and 100, what is the remainder when p^2 is divided by 6?

   (A) 1   (B) 2   (C) 3   (D) 4   (E) 5

14. In 1984, the populations of 1,210 different towns were all different than their populations in 1980. The number of populations that were greater in 1984 than in 1980 was 20 percent greater than the number that were greater in 1980 than in 1984. How many of the towns had a greater population in 1984 than in 1980?

   (A) 242   (B) 363   (C) 550   (D) 660   (E) 847

15. If a two-digit positive integer has its digits reversed, the resulting integer differs from the original by 36. By how much do the two digits differ?

   (A) 3   (B) 4   (C) 5   (D) 6   (E) 7

16. From 1950 to 1960, the value of a certain stock increased 25 percent. From 1960 to 1970, its value decreased 20 percent. What was the overall percent change in the value of the stock from 1950 to 1970?

   (A) –5%   (B) –2.5%   (C) 0%   (D) 2.5%   (E) 5%

A shopper can purchase a bag of tangerines for $6.24, or purchase x tangerines at a cost of $0.24 per tangerine.

Quantity A	Quantity B
17. The greatest possible value of x if the cost of purchasing x tangerines is less than the cost of purchasing the bag	26

18. If c chairs cost d dollars, then at this rate how many dollars will 7 chairs cost?

(A) $7cd$ (B) $\frac{7d}{c}$ (C) $\frac{d}{7c}$ (D) $\frac{7c}{d}$ (E) $\frac{c}{7d}$

Quantity A	Quantity B
19. The sum of every integer from 29 to 89, inclusive	The sum of every integer from 32 to 90, inclusive

20. If $\frac{1}{n} + \frac{1}{n-3} = \frac{1}{n+1}$, then n could be

(A) 3 (B) 1 (C) 0 (D) –1 (E) –2

21. At a recent dinner, John ate 1/3 of the food that he cooked and saved the rest for a later meal. If 1/2 of the food that he ate was vegetables and 3/4 of the food that he saved was not vegetables, what portion of the dinner was not vegetables?

(A) $\frac{1}{6}$ (B) $\frac{1}{4}$ (C) $\frac{1}{3}$ (D) $\frac{2}{3}$ (E) $\frac{5}{6}$

For each town in State S, the number of senior citizens is p percent of the total population. The number of senior citizens in a town whose population is 48,000 is 14,000.

Quantity A	Quantity B
22. The number of senior citizens in a town of 60,000 citizens	16,000

23. The monthly revenue of a certain business was $265,000 for April of this year. If the revenue for the same month last year was $220,000, approximately what was the percent increase in revenue?

    (A) 12% (B) 17% (C) 20% (D) 44% (E) 83%

24. The cost of office space in Town A is $75 per square foot, regardless of footage. In Town B, the cost is $50 per square foot for space up to 50 square feet and twice that for every additional square foot. At what square footage is the cost of office space in Town A identical to that of Town B?

    (A) 50 (B) 75 (C) 100 (D) 125 (E) 150

	Quantity A	Quantity B
25.	4,321(61,840)	4,320(61,841)

26. The present ratio of office workers to managers at a certain company is 30 to 1. If the number of office workers were to increase by 50 and the number of managers were to increase by 5, the ratio of office workers to managers would then be 25 to 1. What is the present number of managers?

    (A) 5 (B) 8 (C) 10 (D) 12 (E) 15

27. $\sqrt{(18)(8)+(36)(12)} =$

    (A) $12\sqrt{3}$ (B) 24 (C) $25\sqrt{2}$ (D) 36 (E) $6\sqrt{18}+8\sqrt{2}$

28. A hardware store charges the same price for each hammer that it sells. If the current price of each hammer were to be increased by $2, 4 fewer hammers could be bought for $160, excluding sales tax. What is the current price, in dollars, of each hammer?

    (A) 2 (B) 8 (C) 10 (D) 12 (E) 16

	Quantity A	Quantity B
29.	$\dfrac{12^4}{2^5 6^3}$	3

30. In the sequence of numbers n_1, n_2, n_3, n_4, n_5, each number after the first is three times the preceding number. If $n_5 - n_3$ is 54, what is the value of n_1?

(A) $\frac{3}{4}$ (B) $\frac{3}{2}$ (C) $\frac{5}{3}$ (D) $\frac{5}{2}$ (E) 3

31. A glass container is 2/5 filled with sodium chloride. A second glass container, which has 4 times the capacity of the smaller container, is 3/8 filled with sodium chloride. If the contents of the smaller container were to be dumped into the larger container, to what fraction of its capacity would the larger container be filled?

(A) $\frac{5}{12}$ (B) $\frac{11}{24}$ (C) $\frac{19}{40}$ (D) $\frac{7}{12}$ (E) $\frac{23}{40}$

32. Which of the following fractions has the greatest value?

(A) $\dfrac{7}{(2^2)(5^2)}$ (B) $\dfrac{3}{(2^3)(5^2)}$ (C) $\dfrac{26}{(2^2)(5^3)}$ (D) $\dfrac{58}{(2^3)(5^3)}$ (E) $\dfrac{110}{(2^4)(5^3)}$

(16) Solutions – Video solutions for each of the previous questions can be found on our website at **www.sherpaprep.com/videos**.

• BOOKMARK this address for future visits!

➤ To view the videos, you'll need the LOGIN and PASSWORD that you created upon registering your copy of <u>Arithmetic & "Plan B" Strategies</u>.

• If you have yet to register your book yet, please go to **www.sherpaprep.com/activate** and enter your email address, last name, and shipping address.

• Be sure to provide the SAME last name and shipping address that you used to purchase your copy of <u>Master Key to the GRE</u> or to enroll in your GRE course with Sherpa Prep!

➤ When checking your answers, we encourage you to watch the solution for any problem that you answered INCORRECTLY

• The same goes for any problem that took you MORE than TWO MINUTES to solve.

• After digesting the explanation, REVISIT your mistake a couple of days later to ensure that the problem no longer poses issues to you.

➤ If you struggle to solve the problem a SECOND time, add it to your "LOG of ERRORS" and redo it every few weeks.

• Solving tricky questions MORE THAN ONCE is the best way to learn from your mistakes and to avoid similar difficulties on your actual exam.

Part I		Part II		
1. D		10. A	20. B	30. A
2. B		11. A	21. D	31. C
3. C		12. C	22. A	32. A
4. C		13. A	23. C	
5. E		14. D	24. C	
6. E		15. B	25. A	
7. A		16. C	26. E	
8. A		17. B	27. B	
9. E		18. B	28. B	
		19. C	29. C	

Chapter 4

Fractions

Fractions

To be discussed:

Fundamental Concepts

Whether you're aiming for a perfect score or a score closer to average, mastery of the following concepts is essential.

1 Introduction
2 Adding and Subtracting Fractions
3 Multiplying Fractions
4 Dividing Fractions
5 Simple vs. Complex Fractions
6 Mixed Numerals
7 Reciprocals
8 The "Comparison Trick"
9 Properties of Zero
10 Fractions Between 0 and 1
11 FUQ's: Fractions with Unspecified Quantities

Rare or Advanced Concepts

The following concepts are either advanced or are tested only on rare occasions. If you don't need an elite math score, don't waste your time!

12 "Multi-Level" Fractions
13 Properties of Numerators and Denominators

Practice Questions

There's no substitute for elbow grease. Practice your new skills to ensure that you internalize what you've studied.

14 Problem Sets
15 Solutions

Fundamental Concepts

(1) Introduction – Like arithmetic, fractions are an important part of the revised GRE.

• Although relatively few questions exclusively involve fractions, many questions require the ability to work with fractions quickly and easily.

➤ Fractions are particularly important for word problems.

• Most word problems can be set up with decimals or with fractions. In most cases, fractions are the smarter choice, since **fractions contain shortcuts that decimals lack**.

• Remember: exam-makers are not interested in your ability to be a human calculator. They're interested in your ability to find smart, simple solutions to problems that seem complex.

➤ Since fractions contain shortcuts that decimals do not, it's often your ability to use fractions confidently that will enable you to find those smart, simple solutions.

• As you likely know, a fraction is a number in the form $\frac{a}{b}$, where the bar separating the a and the b signifies "division".

• The number on top of a fraction is referred to as the **numerator**; the number on bottom of a fraction is referred to as the **denominator**. For example, the fraction $\frac{2}{3}$ has a numerator of 2 and a denominator of 3.

➤ **If the numerator of a fraction is zero, that fraction equals zero.** If the denominator of a fraction is zero, that fraction is considered "undefined".

• Thus, the fraction $\frac{0}{3} = 0$, but the fraction $\frac{3}{0}$ = undefined, because we can't divide by 0.

• Whole numbers can be expressed as fractions by placing the number over 1. Thus, numbers such as 6, 15, and –3 can be represented as $\frac{6}{1}$, $\frac{15}{1}$, and $\frac{-3}{1}$.

➤ When working with fractions, **always be sure to REDUCE your fraction as much as possible.**

• Although $\frac{2}{3}$ and $\frac{6}{9}$ are the same thing, $\frac{2}{3}$ is far easier to work with!

(2) Adding and Subtracting Fractions – To add or subtract fractions, the fractions must have a common denominator.

- Fractions that have the same denominator can be combined by adding or subtracting the **numerators**, while leaving the **denominators** the same. Thus:

$$\frac{1}{5} + \frac{2}{5} = \frac{1+2}{5} = \frac{3}{5} \qquad\qquad \frac{4}{15} - \frac{3}{15} = \frac{4-3}{15} = \frac{1}{15}$$

- If fractions do not have the same denominator, however, they must be GIVEN a COMMON denominator before they can be added or subtracted. To do so:

> Step 1: Look for the smallest number that is cleanly divisible by the denominator of each fraction. This number will be the **least common denominator** (LCD).

- For example, the fractions $\frac{3}{4}$ and $\frac{5}{6}$ have an LCD of 12, since 12 is the smallest number divisible by both 4 and 6.

> Step 2: **Multiply** the numerator <u>AND</u> the denominator of each fraction by the value that raises each denominator to the LCD.

- This will convert each fraction to an EQUIVALENT fraction over the new LCD. For example, $\frac{3}{4}$ converts to $\frac{9}{12}$, since multiplying the top and bottom by 3 gives us:

$$\frac{3}{4} = \frac{3(3)}{4(3)} = \frac{9}{12}$$

> ➢ Thus, to add two fractions such as $\frac{2}{9}$ and $\frac{1}{4}$, we first need to find their LCD. The LCD of 9 and 4 is 36, since 36 is the smallest number divisible by 9 and 4.

- Then, we need to convert each fraction to an equivalent fraction with a denominator of 36. In the case of $\frac{2}{9}$ and $\frac{1}{4}$, those fractions are $\frac{8}{36}$ and $\frac{9}{36}$, respectively, since:

$$\frac{2}{9} = \frac{2(4)}{9(4)} = \frac{8}{36} \qquad \text{and} \qquad \frac{1}{4} = \frac{1(9)}{4(9)} = \frac{9}{36}$$

- Thus, $\frac{2}{9} + \frac{1}{4}$ equals $\frac{17}{36}$, since:

COMBINE the
numerators

$$\frac{2}{9} + \frac{1}{4} \;\rightarrow\; \frac{2(4)}{9(4)} + \frac{1(9)}{4(9)} \;\rightarrow\; \frac{8}{36} + \frac{9}{36} \;\rightarrow\; \frac{8+9}{36} = \boxed{\frac{17}{36}}$$

CONVERT
each fraction

➤ There is also a VERY effective shortcut you can use to add or subtract two fractions. We call it the $\boxed{\textbf{Fast Fraction Shortcut}}$.

• To use this shortcut, simply CROSS-MULTIPLY the two fractions and ADD (or SUBTRACT) their products. Then place the sum (or difference) over the PRODUCT of the denominators.

• For example, to add $\frac{2}{9}+\frac{1}{4}$, first cross-multiply them as follows:

$$\frac{2}{9} \diagup\!\!\!\!\!\diagdown \frac{1}{4}$$

➤ Then place the sum of the products over 9×4, which is 36. Since $4 \times 2 = \boxed{8}$ and $9 \times 1 = \boxed{9}$, these fractions add to $\frac{8+9}{36}$, or $\frac{17}{36}$.

• Likewise, to subtract $\frac{1}{7}-\frac{2}{5}$, first cross-multiply them as follows:

$$\frac{1}{7} \diagup\!\!\!\!\!\diagdown \frac{2}{5}$$

• Then, place the difference of the products over 7×5, which is 35. Since $5 \times 1 = \boxed{5}$ and $7 \times 2 = \boxed{14}$, these fractions subtract to $\frac{5-14}{35}$, or $-\frac{9}{35}$.

➤ When combining WHOLE NUMBERS and FRACTIONS, it can be helpful to **place the whole number over 1** to avoid confusion!

• For example, to subtract $4-\frac{3}{5}$, let $4=\frac{4}{1}$ and cross-multiply the two fractions as follows:

$$\frac{4}{1} \diagup\!\!\!\!\!\diagdown \frac{3}{5}$$

• Then place the difference of the products over 1×5, which is 5. Since $5 \times 4 = \boxed{20}$ and $1 \times 3 = \boxed{3}$, these fractions subtract to $\frac{20-3}{5}$, or $\frac{17}{5}$.

➤ Likewise, to subtract $3-\frac{5}{8}$, let $3=\frac{3}{1}$ and cross-multiply the two fractions as follows:

$$\frac{3}{1} \diagup\!\!\!\!\!\diagdown \frac{5}{8}$$

• Then place the difference of the products over 1×8, which is 8. Since $8 \times 3 = \boxed{24}$ and $1 \times 5 = \boxed{5}$, these fractions subtract to $\frac{24-5}{8}$, or $\frac{19}{8}$.

(3) Multiplying Fractions – Of everything you need to know about fractions, perhaps nothing is more important than how to multiply them properly.

- On the most basic level, multiplying fractions is easy.

  ➤ To multiply two or more fractions: simply multiply the numerators together, then multiply the denominators.

- For example, $\frac{2}{3} \times \frac{4}{5} = \frac{8}{15}$ since:

$$\frac{2}{3} \times \frac{4}{5} = \frac{2(4)}{3(5)} = \frac{8}{15}$$

  ➤ Unfortunately, things can get more complicated in a hurry.

- Imagine that you needed to multiply $\frac{14}{15} \times \frac{18}{42}$.

- If you were to multiply these fractions in the manner suggested above, not only would **the process be time-consuming**, but the results would be large and hard to work with.

  ➤ The key to multiplying fractions is to BREAK them DOWN before you multiply.

- By breaking numerators and denominators into simple elements, their COMMON elements become easy to CANCEL. Better still, the resulting math becomes dramatically easier.

- Thus, $\frac{14}{15} \times \frac{18}{42} = \frac{2}{5}$, since:

The tops and bottoms of these fractions have a 3, 6, and 7 in common

$$\frac{14}{15} \times \frac{18}{42} \;\rightarrow\; \frac{2(7)}{3(5)} \cdot \frac{3(6)}{6(7)} \;\rightarrow\; \frac{2(\cancel{7})}{\cancel{3}(5)} \cdot \frac{\cancel{3}(\cancel{6})}{\cancel{6}(\cancel{7})} = \frac{2}{5}$$

  ➤ If you're not sure how to break down the numbers you've been given, simply ask yourself "**what multiplies to this number?**"

- For example, if one of your fractions contains the number 48, ask yourself "what multiplies to 48?"

- It doesn't matter whether you think of 6×8, 4×12, or 2×24: **as long as your numbers multiply to the number in question, you can't go wrong.**

➤ It can also be helpful to **look for common factors**.

• Imagine that you needed to multiply $\frac{48}{10} \times \frac{15}{18}$.

• Because one of the numerators contains the number 48, it may prove faster to break down 48 as $\boxed{6} \times 8$ (rather than 4×12 or 2×24), since one of the denominators contains an 18, which is the product of $\boxed{6} \times 3$.

➤ Ideally, therefore, you would choose to break down the numbers as follows before multiplying them:

$$\frac{48}{10} \times \frac{15}{18} \rightarrow \frac{\cancel{6}(8)}{2(\cancel{5})} \cdot \frac{\cancel{5}(\cancel{3})}{\cancel{3}(\cancel{6})} = \frac{8}{2} = 4$$

• To be clear, **you will get the same result no matter how you break down the numbers.** Ignoring obvious common factors, however, does create a bit more work. Hence, if you break down 48 as 4×12, the multiplication might look like this:

$$\frac{48}{10} \times \frac{15}{18} \rightarrow \frac{4(12)}{2(\cancel{5})} \cdot \frac{\cancel{5}(\cancel{3})}{\cancel{3}(6)} \rightarrow \frac{4(\cancel{2})(\cancel{6})}{\cancel{2}} \cdot \frac{1}{\cancel{6}} = 4$$

➤ Above all, always remember one thing: when multiplying fractions, **never make the numbers bigger**, unless you have to after everything's been canceled out.

• Doing so is always a mistake that will erase shortcuts, create more work, and cause you to make computational errors. Consider the following:

What is the value of $\frac{14}{9} \times \frac{5}{4} \times \frac{18}{7}$?

(A) 1 (B) 2 (C) 3 (D) 4 (E) 5

Answer: E. Although you can multiply $14 \times 5 \times 18$ and divide the result by $9 \times 4 \times 7$, doing so only increases the difficulty of the problem.

➤ Remember: **exam-makers have zero interest in your ability to be a human calculator**, and the calculator they provide is cumbersome to use.

• On the contrary, they're interested in your ability to find smart solutions. Breaking down numbers is ALWAYS a step in the right direction. Here, it proves the answer to be (E), since:

$$\frac{14}{9} \times \frac{5}{4} \times \frac{18}{7} \rightarrow \frac{\cancel{2}(\cancel{7})}{\cancel{9}} \times \frac{5}{\cancel{2}(\cancel{2})} \times \frac{\cancel{2}(\cancel{9})}{\cancel{7}} = 5$$

Chapter 4: Fractions

(4) Dividing Fractions – The easiest way to divide two fractions is to flip the second fraction and to multiply the two together.

• In other words, division is simply another form of multiplication.

➢ So, once you flip the second fraction, be sure to **break down your numbers** before you multiply.

• Breaking the numerators and denominators into smaller numbers will make their common elements easy to cancel and the resulting math dramatically easier.

$$\text{If } x = \frac{4}{25} \div \frac{8}{15}, \text{ what is the value of } x?$$

(A) $\frac{1}{10}$ (B) $\frac{2}{9}$ (C) $\frac{3}{10}$ (D) $\frac{3}{8}$ (E) $\frac{2}{5}$

Answer. C. To divide $\frac{4}{25}$ by $\frac{8}{15}$, we simply need to flip $\frac{8}{15}$ and then multiply the two fractions. Breaking down the numbers before multiplying will keep the math easy:

$$\frac{4}{25} \div \frac{8}{15} \rightarrow \frac{4}{25} \cdot \frac{15}{8} \rightarrow \frac{\cancel{4}}{5(\cancel{5})} \cdot \frac{3(\cancel{5})}{2(\cancel{4})} = \frac{3}{10}$$

• Thus, the correct is (C).

➢ If you have more than one instance of division, be sure to follow the order of operations (PEMDAS).

Quantity A	**Quantity B**
$\frac{21}{9} \div \frac{5}{18} \div \frac{14}{15}$	10

Answer. B. According to the order of operations (PEMDAS), we always work left to right when handling identical operations. Here, since we have two instances of division, let's transform the leftmost instance of division first:

$$\frac{21}{9} \div \frac{5}{18} \div \frac{14}{15} \rightarrow \frac{21}{9} \cdot \frac{18}{5} \div \frac{14}{15}$$

• Next, let's transform the remaining instance of division and break down our numbers. Doing so proves that Quantity B is greater than Quantity A, since:

$$\frac{21}{9} \cdot \frac{18}{5} \div \frac{14}{15} \rightarrow \frac{21}{9} \cdot \frac{18}{5} \cdot \frac{15}{14} \rightarrow \frac{3(\cancel{7})}{\cancel{9}} \cdot \frac{\cancel{9}(\cancel{2})}{\cancel{5}} \cdot \frac{3(\cancel{5})}{\cancel{2}(\cancel{7})} = 3 \cdot 3 = 9$$

• Thus, the correct is (B).

138

Sherpa Prep

➢ Another way that exam-makers can test your ability to divide fractions is with **"fractions containing fractions"**.

• By the term "fractions containing fractions" we simply mean any fraction that has a fraction for its numerator or denominator (or both):

$$\dfrac{\frac{3}{5}}{4} \qquad \dfrac{\frac{2}{5}}{\frac{3}{8}} \qquad \dfrac{7}{\frac{2}{9}}$$

• For example, all of the fractions above would both be considered "fractions containing fractions" since each of them has a fraction for its numerator or denominator (or both).

➢ To simplify such fractions, simply **multiply the numerator by the "flip" of the denominator.** Thus:

$$\dfrac{\frac{2}{5}}{\frac{3}{8}} = \frac{2}{5} \times \frac{8}{3} = \frac{16}{15} \qquad\qquad \dfrac{\frac{3}{4}}{\frac{7}{5}} = \frac{3}{4} \times \frac{5}{7} = \frac{15}{28}$$

• If either your numerator or your denominator is a whole number, it can be helpful to put that whole number over 1:

$$\dfrac{6}{\frac{2}{3}} = \dfrac{\frac{6}{1}}{\frac{2}{3}} = \frac{6}{1} \times \frac{3}{2} = 9 \qquad\qquad \dfrac{\frac{4}{7}}{4} = \dfrac{\frac{4}{7}}{\frac{4}{1}} = \frac{4}{7} \times \frac{1}{4} = \frac{1}{7}$$

➢ Consider the following:

$$\dfrac{\frac{a}{b}}{c} \cdot \dfrac{c}{\frac{a}{b}} \text{ is equal to which of the following?}$$

(A) 1 (B) $\frac{a}{b}$ **(C)** abc **(D)** $\frac{a^2}{b^2}$ **(E)** c^2

Answer: A. When solving intimidating or confusing problems, it's always helpful to break them down one step at a time. As a start, let's simplify each fraction by multiplying their numerator by the "flip" of their denominators:

$$\dfrac{\frac{a}{b}}{c} \;\rightarrow\; \frac{a}{b} \cdot \frac{1}{c} = \frac{a}{bc} \qquad\qquad \dfrac{c}{\frac{a}{b}} \;\rightarrow\; \frac{c}{1} \cdot \frac{b}{a} = \frac{cb}{a}$$

• Then, let's multiply the two fractions together. Doing so proves the answer to be (A), as:

$$\frac{a}{bc} \cdot \frac{cb}{a} \;\rightarrow\; \frac{\cancel{a}}{bc} \cdot \frac{cb}{\cancel{a}} \;\rightarrow\; \frac{bc}{bc} = 1$$

Chapter 4: Fractions

(5) Simple vs. Complex Fractions – Any fraction that contains addition or subtraction can be referred to as a complex fraction.

- Thus, fractions such as $\frac{1+2}{6}$ and $\frac{8}{4-2}$ would be considered COMPLEX, since each contains addition or subtraction.

- Conversely, fractions such as $\frac{4 \times 8}{2}$ and $\frac{8}{2 \div 2}$ would be considered SIMPLE, since neither contains addition or subtraction.

  ➤ The distinction between simple and complex fractions is an important one. As we saw earlier, terms within a simple fraction can be broken down and canceled out.

- In the case of a complex fraction, however, **the ADDITION or SUBTRACTION should ALWAYS be carried out** before we break down or cancel out any terms, like so:

$$\frac{8+6}{4-2} = \frac{14}{2} = 7 \qquad\qquad \frac{8(4+6)}{4} = \frac{8(10)}{4} = 20$$

- If we break down or cancel out terms in a complex fraction BEFORE we carry out the addition or subtraction, we can get the WRONG result. Thus:

<table>
<tr><td align="center"><u>WRONG</u></td><td align="center"><u>RIGHT</u></td></tr>
<tr><td align="center">$\frac{4+8}{2+2} = \frac{2(\cancel{2})+4(\cancel{2})}{\cancel{2}+\cancel{2}} = 6$</td><td align="center">$\frac{4+8}{2+2} = \frac{12}{4} = 3$</td></tr>
</table>

  ➤ When working with complex fractions, there's a very effective shortcut you can use to simplify the arithmetic. We call it $\boxed{\textbf{The Complex Numerator Shortcut}}$.

- If the NUMERATOR of a complex fraction contains addition or subtraction, that fraction can be split as follows:

$$\frac{1+2}{6} \quad\rightarrow\quad \frac{1}{6}+\frac{2}{6} \quad\rightarrow\quad \frac{3}{6}=\frac{1}{2}$$

- The same is **not true** for fractions with complex DENOMINATORS. Such fractions CANNOT be split:

<table>
<tr><td align="center"><u>WRONG</u></td><td align="center"><u>RIGHT</u></td></tr>
<tr><td align="center">$\frac{16}{4+8} = \frac{16}{4}+\frac{16}{8} = 4+2 = 6$</td><td align="center">$\frac{16}{4+8} = \frac{16}{12} = \frac{4(\cancel{4})}{3(\cancel{4})} = \frac{4}{3}$</td></tr>
</table>

- At first glance, this technique may not seem like much of a shortcut, but it can be extremely effective with difficult fractions:

$$\text{What is the value of } \frac{9,999^2 + 9,999}{9,999}\text{?}$$

(A) 10 **(B)** 99 **(C)** 100 **(D)** 9,999 **(E)** 10,000

Answer. E. Although it may be tempting to solve this problem with a calculator, remember: **the GRE calculator can be difficult to use and is therefore slow**. Further, the GRE calculator cannot compute very big (or small) numbers such as $9,999^2$.

➢ To solve this problem quickly and easily, first note that our fraction has a **complex numerator**. Any fraction with a complex numerator can be split as follows:

$$\frac{9,999^2 + 9,999}{9,999} \quad \rightarrow \quad \frac{9,999^2}{9,999} + \frac{9,999}{9,999}$$

- Next, notice that $\frac{9,999^2}{9,999} = \frac{9,999 \cdot \cancel{9,999}}{\cancel{9,999}}$, which cancels to 9,999. And since $\frac{9,999}{9,999} = 1$, the answer must be (E), as:

$$\frac{9,999^2}{9,999} + \frac{9,999}{9,999} \quad \rightarrow \quad 9,999 + 1 = 10,000$$

➢ Let's take a look at a second example:

$$\text{If } \frac{b}{a} = \frac{1}{3}, \text{ what is the value of } \frac{a+b}{b}\text{?}$$

$$\frac{3+1}{1} \qquad 3+1 = 4$$

(A) $\frac{1}{9}$ **(B)** 1 **(C)** $2\frac{1}{3}$ **(D)** 4 **(E)** $4\frac{2}{3}$

Answer. D. Because $\frac{a+b}{b}$ has a complex numerator, we can separate it as follows:

$$\frac{a+b}{b} \quad \rightarrow \quad \frac{a}{b} + \frac{b}{b}$$

- Further, since $\frac{b}{a} = \frac{1}{3}$, the value of $\frac{a}{b}$ must be $\frac{3}{1} = 3$. Finally, since $\frac{b}{b} = 1$, the value of $\frac{a+b}{b}$ must be 4, as:

$$\frac{a+b}{b} \quad \rightarrow \quad \frac{a}{b} + \frac{b}{b} \quad \rightarrow \quad 3 + 1 = 4$$

- Thus, the correct answer is (D).

Chapter 4: Fractions

(6) Mixed Numerals – The addition of a whole number to a fraction creates a mixed numeral.

$$1 + \frac{2}{3} = 1\frac{2}{3} \qquad\qquad 8 + \frac{3}{5} = 8\frac{3}{5}$$

• In other words, notation such as $3\frac{1}{2}$ is really shorthand for $3 + \frac{1}{2}$. Thus, to convert a mixed numeral into a fraction, simply **express the whole number as a fraction**:

$$3\frac{1}{2} \;\rightarrow\; 3 + \frac{1}{2} \;\rightarrow\; \frac{6}{2} + \frac{1}{2} = \frac{7}{2}$$

• You can also convert mixed numerals to fractions by **multiplying the denominator and the whole number, then adding the numerator**. Just remember to place the result over the denominator:

$$3\frac{1}{2} = \frac{2(3) + 1}{2} = \frac{7}{2} \qquad\qquad 8\frac{3}{5} = \frac{5(8) + 3}{5} = \frac{43}{5}$$

 ➤ **To convert a fraction into a mixed numeral,** first divide the numerator by the numerator. Then place the remainder over the denominator:

$$\frac{7}{2} = 3 \text{ remainder } 1 \;\rightarrow\; 3\frac{1}{2} \qquad\qquad \frac{43}{5} = 8 \text{ remainder } 3 \;\rightarrow\; 8\frac{3}{5}$$

• Mixed numerals contain no shortcuts and can be difficult to add, subtract, multiply, or divide. Fractions, on the other hand, contain numerous shortcuts and are easy to combine.

 ➤ When adding, subtracting, multiplying, or dividing mixed numerals, **always convert your mixed numerals into fractions** before performing the operation!

Quantity A	**Quantity B**
$1\frac{3}{5} \div 1\frac{1}{15}$	$1\frac{1}{2}$

Answer: C. To solve this question, let's first convert each mixed numeral into a fraction:

$$1\frac{3}{5} = \frac{5(1) + 3}{5} = \frac{8}{5} \qquad\qquad 1\frac{1}{15} = \frac{15(1) + 1}{15} = \frac{16}{15}$$

• Then let's flip the second fraction and break down the numbers before multiplying. Doing so proves that the correct answer is (C), since:

$$\frac{8}{5} \div \frac{16}{15} \;\rightarrow\; \frac{8}{5} \cdot \frac{15}{16} \;\rightarrow\; \frac{\cancel{8}}{\cancel{5}} \cdot \frac{3(\cancel{5})}{2(\cancel{8})} = \frac{3}{2} = 1\frac{1}{2}$$

(7) Reciprocals – Any two numbers **whose product equals positive 1** are reciprocals.

- For example, 2 and $\frac{1}{2}$ are considered reciprocals, as $2 \times \frac{1}{2} = 1$. Likewise, $\frac{3}{4}$ and $\frac{4}{3}$ are also considered reciprocals, as $\frac{3}{4} \times \frac{4}{3} = 1$.

  ➤ While reciprocals are commonly thought of as "flips" of one another, it is important to understand that SOME reciprocals are NOT "flips".

- Note, for example, that $\frac{1}{\sqrt{3}}$ and $\frac{3}{\sqrt{3}}$ may not look like "flips", but they are reciprocals, as their product equals 1:

$$\frac{1}{\sqrt{3}} \cdot \frac{3}{\sqrt{3}} = \frac{3}{3} = 1$$

  ➤ It is also important to understand that a fraction may have MORE than ONE reciprocal.

- Note, for example, that $\sqrt{3}$ is ALSO a reciprocal of $\frac{1}{\sqrt{3}}$, since their product equals positive 1:

$$\frac{1}{\sqrt{3}} \cdot \frac{\sqrt{3}}{1} = \frac{\sqrt{3}}{\sqrt{3}} = 1$$

  ➤ When working with questions that involve reciprocals, NEVER make assumptions. Always multiply your terms together to see whether they equal positive 1.

- Consider the following:

Which of the following values are reciprocals?

Select all such values.

A $\frac{\sqrt{5}}{3}$ and $\frac{3\sqrt{5}}{5}$ B $-\frac{21}{6}$ and $\frac{2}{7}$ C $\sqrt{9}$ and $\frac{1}{3}$

Answer: A, C. $\frac{\sqrt{5}}{3}$ and $\frac{3\sqrt{5}}{5}$ are reciprocals, as are $\sqrt{9}$ and $\frac{1}{3}$, since their products equal 1:

$$\frac{\sqrt{5}}{\cancel{3}} \cdot \frac{\cancel{3}\sqrt{5}}{5} \rightarrow \frac{\sqrt{5} \cdot \sqrt{5}}{5} = \frac{5}{5} = 1 \qquad \sqrt{9} \cdot \frac{1}{3} \rightarrow 3 \cdot \frac{1}{3} = \frac{3}{3} = 1$$

- The product of $-\frac{21}{6}$ and $\frac{2}{7}$, however, equals –1, so they are NOT reciprocals:

$$-\frac{21}{6} \cdot \frac{2}{7} = -\frac{\cancel{3}(\cancel{7})}{\cancel{3}(\cancel{2})} \cdot \frac{\cancel{2}}{\cancel{7}} = -1$$

Chapter 4: Fractions

(8) The "Comparison Trick" – Almost as important as your ability to multiply fractions is your ability to compare fractions.

• Comparisons are a big part of GRE math. On every exam, 15 of the 40 math questions are Quantitative Comparison questions.

➤ Since many of those 15 questions will end in the comparison of two fractions, it's important that you be able to do so quickly.

• Fortunately, there's a very easy way to compare two fractions. We call it the
⎧ **Comparison Trick** ⎫.

• To compare two fractions, simply cross-multiply their numerators and denominators.

➤ Multiply from the BOTTOM UP, and write each product OVER the corresponding numerator, as shown below.

• **The fraction under the LARGER product will ALWAYS be the larger fraction.** For example:

$\frac{4}{9}$ is larger than $\frac{3}{7}$, since: $\frac{5}{11}$ is larger than $\frac{4}{9}$, since:

27   28   **45   44**
$\frac{3}{7}$ ⤫ $\frac{4}{9}$ $\frac{5}{11}$ ⤫ $\frac{4}{9}$

• Why does this technique work? Reconsider the last example. To compare $\frac{5}{11}$ and $\frac{4}{9}$ formally, we first need to determine their LCD, which is 99.

➤ We then need to convert them to equivalent fractions over the LCD, as follows:

$$\frac{5}{11} = \frac{5(9)}{11(9)} = \frac{45}{99} \qquad \frac{4}{9} = \frac{4(11)}{9(11)} = \frac{44}{99}$$

• Since $\frac{45}{99}$ has "more 99ths" than $\frac{44}{99}$ (in the same way $\frac{2}{3}$ has "more 3rds" than $\frac{1}{3}$), $\frac{5}{11}$ is larger than $\frac{4}{9}$.

• By cross-multiplying 9 × 5 to get 45 and 11 × 4 to get 44, we are simply determining the numerator of each fraction without the laborious task of converting each fraction to an equivalent fraction over the LCD.

(9) Properties of Zero – As mentioned in the introduction, fractions that contain zeroes have two special properties:

I. If the **numerator** of a fraction is zero, that fraction equals zero. Thus, a fraction such as $\frac{0}{5} = 0$, since its numerator equals zero.

II. If the **denominator** of a fraction is zero, that fraction is considered UNDEFINED. Thus, a fraction such as $\frac{5}{0}$ = undefined, since its denominator equals zero.

➤ Many problems contain RESTRICTIONS such as $x \neq -a$, $ab \neq 0$, and $xy > 0$.

• Such restrictions often look intimidating and seem to add complexity to the problems in which they appear.

• In most cases, however, these sorts of restrictions simply indicate that the problem contains a fraction and that the denominator of a fraction cannot equal zero.

➤ In other words, such restrictions serve to CLOSE potential LOOPHOLES in a problem.

• They are technicalities that must be stated, but they add no further difficulties to their problems.

• Consider the following:

If $a + b \neq 0$ the reciprocal of $a + b$ equals

(A) $\frac{1}{a+b}$ (B) $\frac{1}{a}+\frac{1}{b}$ (C) $\frac{b+a}{a+b}$ (D) $\frac{1}{a-b}$ (E) $\frac{b-a}{a+b}$

Answer. A. To determine the reciprocal of $a + b$, we must combine a and b into a single term in order to flip it. By writing a and b as fractions, we can do so as follows:

$$a+b=\frac{a}{1}+\frac{b}{1}=\frac{a+b}{1} \xrightarrow{\text{flip!}} \frac{1}{a+b}$$

• Looking back at the question, notice that $a + b \neq 0$ since $\frac{1}{a+b}$ would be **undefined** if $a + b$ were to equal zero.

(10) Fractions Between 0 and 1 – Any fraction between 0 and 1 is known as a proper fraction.

• Proper fractions are EXTREMELY important for the GRE, since they have a very special property.

> ➤ In short: such fractions, when MULTIPLIED with or DIVIDED against positive values, produce the OPPOSITE results of numbers <u>larger</u> than 1. For example:

• **Multiplying** a positive value by a number larger than 1 makes the value bigger. Multiplying a positive value by a fraction between 0 and 1, however, makes that value smaller.

$$\text{Larger than 1: } \boxed{10} \times 2 \rightarrow \boxed{20} \qquad \text{Proper Fraction: } \boxed{10} \times \tfrac{1}{2} \rightarrow \boxed{5}$$

• **Dividing** a positive value by a number larger than 1 makes that value smaller. Dividing a positive value by a fraction between 0 and 1, however, makes that value bigger.

$$\text{Larger than 1: } \boxed{10} \div 2 \rightarrow \boxed{5} \qquad \text{Proper Fraction: } \boxed{10} \div \tfrac{1}{2} \rightarrow \boxed{20}$$

> ➤ Likewise, the SQUARES and SQUARE ROOTS of fractions between 0 and 1 also behave in the OPPOSITE manner of other <u>positive</u> squares and square roots:

• **Squaring** a positive value larger than 1 makes that value bigger. Squaring a fraction between 0 and 1, however, makes that fraction smaller.

$$\text{Larger than 1: } 10^2 \rightarrow \boxed{100} \qquad \text{Proper Fraction: } \left(\tfrac{1}{2}\right)^2 \rightarrow \boxed{\tfrac{1}{4}}$$

• **Taking the Square Root** of a positive value larger than 1 makes that value smaller. Taking the square root of a fraction between 0 and 1, however, makes that fraction bigger.

$$\text{Larger than 1: } \sqrt{4} \rightarrow \boxed{2} \qquad \text{Proper Fraction: } \sqrt{\tfrac{1}{2}} \rightarrow \boxed{\cong 0.71}$$

> ➤ Many questions test this concept specifically. The difficulty of such questions can be GREATLY reduced if you RECOGNIZE the concept rather than compute the numbers.

• Consider the following:

Answer: A. Although we can solve this problem by computing the values of both quantities, note that doing so would be time-consuming, since the values of 5^6 and 5^7 are difficult to calculate.

> Note also that the GRE calculator would be of little help here, since it cannot compute exponents and is generally awkward to use.

• To solve this problem quickly, we simply need to recognize that **the more we multiply a fraction between 0 and 1, the smaller it gets!** Thus, $(1/5)^6$ must be greater than $(1/5)^7$, since $(1/5)^6$ requires us to multiply 1/5 six times, while $(1/5)^7$ requires us to multiply 1/5 seven times.

• A second example:

Quantity A	**Quantity B**
$\sqrt[3]{\dfrac{2}{7}}$	$\left(\dfrac{3}{11}\right)^3$

Answer: A. As with the previous problem, we might be tempted to solve this by calculator. However, it would again be of little help since the GRE calculator cannot compute cube roots or exponents.

> To solve this problem, we only need to recognize that 2/7 is larger than 3/11 by using the "Comparison Trick":

$$\overset{\displaystyle 22}{\frac{2}{7}} \ \diagdown\hspace{-1.0em}\diagup \ \overset{\displaystyle 21}{\frac{3}{11}}$$

• Since 2/7 is a number between 0 and 1, **its cube root will be even larger than 2/7**, as taking the root of such numbers makes them bigger.

• Conversely, 3/11 is also a number between 0 and 1, so **its cube will be even smaller than 3/11**, since the more we multiply fractions between 0 and 1, the smaller they get. Thus, since 2/7 is originally bigger than 3/11, and then gets even bigger while 3/11 gets even smaller, Quantity A must be larger than Quantity B.

(11) FUQ's: Fractions with Unspecified Quantities – Previously, in our discussion of "Plan B" Strategies, we introduced a type of problem that we like to call "FUQ's".

• As you may recall, the term "FUQ" is an acronym that is short for "**Fraction** problems with **Unspecified Quantities**." In that discussion, we suggested that the key to solving FUQ's is to pick numbers.

➤ Specifically, we recommended that you **pick a number equal to the PRODUCT of EVERY denominator** in the problem.

• To recall the strategy properly, let's work through a practice problem:

Adam ate $\frac{1}{3}$ of a pie, and Billy ate $\frac{1}{4}$ of what Adam did not. If Cletus eats $\frac{1}{2}$ of the remaining pie, what fraction of the pie is left?

(A) $\frac{1}{9}$ (B) $\frac{1}{8}$ (C) $\frac{1}{6}$ (D) $\frac{1}{4}$ (E) $\frac{3}{8}$

Answer. D. This problem contains fractional quantities, but no actual values. Thus, we can pick numbers. Let's pretend that the pie consists of 24 identical slices.

➤ Why choose 24? When solving FUQ's, you always want to **pick a number equal to the product of every denominator**, and here that number equals $3 \times 4 \times 2$, or 24.

• If Adam eats 1/3 of those 24 slices, then Adam eats 8 slices and leaves 16, since 1/3 of 24 is 8. And if Billy eats 1/4 of what **Adam does not**, then Billy eats 4 slices and leaves 12, since 1/4 of 16 is 4.

• Finally, if Cletus eats 1/2 of **what Adam and Billy do not**, Cletus must eat 6 of the remaining 12 slices. Because Cletus leaves 6 slices, and the pie originally had 24 slices, the correct answer is (D), since 6/24 = 1/4.

➤ The reason we choose numbers to solve FUQ's is that doing so makes the math easy.

• We could solve problems like the one above by assigning variables to the unknown values. Picking numbers, however, eliminates the need to set up equations and is therefore faster.

• As mentioned, be sure to pick a number equal to the product of EVERY denominator, **NOT the least common denominator** (LCD). The two may seem like the same thing, but this is not always the case. For example, 4 and 8 have a product of 32 but an LCD of 8, since 8 is divisible by both 4 and 8.

> ➤ Picking a number equal to the product of the denominators will ensure that your problem breaks down into **simple whole numbers** that are easy to work with.

- Although you can choose numbers other than the product of the denominator, doing so will likely leave you with awkward or impossible amounts that may confuse you. And the same is often true of picking the LCD.

- Consider the following:

2/3 of the students in a certain class are right-handed, and 5/6 of the left-handed students have blonde hair. If none of the right-handed students have blonde hair, and no student is ambidextrous, what fraction of the class has blonde hair?

$$(A) \; \frac{1}{4} \quad (B) \; \frac{5}{18} \quad (C) \; \frac{1}{3} \quad (D) \; \frac{2}{5} \quad (E) \; \frac{4}{9}$$

Answer. B. This problem contains fractional quantities but no actual values. Thus, we can pick numbers. To illustrate the point above, let's **mistakenly** pick the LCD of 2/3 and 5/6 to solve the problem.

> ➤ Since 3 and 6 have an LCD of 6, let's pretend that the class has 6 students.

- If 2/3 of those students are right-handed, then **the class has 4 right-handed students and 2 left-handed students**, since no student is ambidextrous and 2/3 of 6 = 4.

- However, if the class only has 2 left-handed students and 5/6 of those students are blonde, then the problem no longer makes sense: how are we supposed to determine 5/6 of 2 students?

> ➤ To solve this problem correctly, let's pick the product of the denominators. Since 3 and 6 have a product of 18, let's instead pretend that the class has 18 students.

- If 2/3 of those students are right-handed, then **the class has 12 right-handed students and 6 left-handed students**, since 2/3 of 18 = 12 (and no student is ambidextrous).

- And, if 5/6 of the left-handed students are blonde, then 5 of the left-handed students have blonde hair and 1 does not, since 5/6 of 6 = 5.

> ➤ According to the problem, **no right-handed student has blonde hair** and no students are ambidextrous.

- Thus, the class only has 5 blonde students in total. Since there are 18 students in the class and only 5 of them are blonde, the correct answer must be (B).

➤ On rare occasions, you may notice a "FUQ" that involves real numbers.

• Unfortunately, **if your question involves REAL numbers, you CAN'T pick numbers**. To understand why, consider the following problem:

2/5 of the movies at a certain rental shop are dramas, 1/4 are mysteries, 1/3 are comedies, and the rest are horror. If the rental shop has 80 horror movies, how many movies does the rental shop have?

(A) 2,400   (B) 2,800   (C) 3,600   (D) 4,200   (E) 4,800

Answer. E. Although the number of movies at the shop is unspecified, it's clear that the total is at least PARTIALLY specified, since it **includes 80 horror movies**.

➤ Thus, we cannot choose numbers here. If we were to invent our own imaginary number, it might contradict the information given to us.

• To solve problems like this, simply let the total = x. Since dramas are 2/5 of that total, mysteries 1/4, and comedies 1/3, we can say:

$$\text{dramas} = \frac{2}{5}x \qquad \text{mysteries} = \frac{1}{4}x \qquad \text{comedies} = \frac{1}{3}x$$

• Further, since the dramas + the mysteries + the comedies + the 80 horror movies = the total number of movies, we can say:

$$\frac{2}{5}x + \frac{1}{4}x + \frac{1}{3}x + 80 = x$$

➤ Finally, we can add the fractions and solve for x as follows, thereby proving that the rental shop has a total of 4,800 movies:

$\frac{24}{60}x + \frac{15}{60}x + \frac{20}{60}x + 80 = x$	Convert the fractions to an LCD of 60.
$\frac{59}{60}x + 80 = x$	Add the fractions.
$\frac{59}{60}x + 80 = \frac{60}{60}x$	Convert x to $\frac{60}{60}x$.
$80 = \frac{1}{60}x$	Subtract $\frac{60}{60}x - \frac{59}{60}x$.
$4,800 = x$	Multiply both sides by 60.

• As we'll see later on, there are faster ways to do the algebra. Until then, however, remember: **you CAN'T pick numbers if your "FUQ" has REAL numbers**.

Rare or Advanced Concepts

(12) "Multi-Level" Fractions – Complex fractions that contain fractions in either the numerator or the denominator can be thought of as having **multiple "levels"**.

- A "level" typically consists of two terms that need to be added or subtracted.

  ➤ For example, the fraction on the left has a bottom "level" of $2+\frac{1}{3}$, while that on the right has a bottom "level" of $4+\frac{1}{5}$:

$$\frac{1}{2+\frac{1}{3}} \qquad \frac{3}{4+\frac{1}{5}}$$

- To simplify such fractions, **rewrite them one "level" at a time**, starting with the **bottom** "level" and progressing upwards:

$$\frac{1}{2+\frac{1}{3}} \to \frac{1}{2\frac{1}{3}} \to \frac{1}{\frac{7}{3}} \qquad\qquad \frac{3}{4+\frac{1}{5}} \to \frac{3}{4\frac{1}{5}} \to \frac{3}{\frac{21}{5}}$$

  ➤ Once the "bottom" level can no longer be simplified, multiply the top of the fraction by the "flip" of the bottom:

$$\frac{1}{\frac{7}{3}} \to 1\cdot\frac{3}{7} \to \frac{3}{7} \qquad\qquad \frac{3}{\frac{21}{5}} \to 3\cdot\frac{5}{21} \to \cancel{3}\cdot\frac{5}{\cancel{21}}=\frac{5}{7}$$

- To ensure that you've got it, let's work through a trickier example together. Consider the following:

The expression $\dfrac{a}{d+\frac{b}{c}}$ is equivalent to which of the following?

(A) $\dfrac{ac}{cd+b}$ **(B)** $\dfrac{bc}{ad+c}$ **(C)** $\dfrac{cd+b}{ad}$ **(D)** $\dfrac{ac+b}{cd}$ **(E)** $\dfrac{a}{cd+bc}$

Answer. A. Despite its appearance, this fraction is no more difficult than the examples above. To start, simplify the "bottom level":

$$\frac{a}{d+\frac{b}{c}} \to \frac{a}{d\frac{b}{c}} \to \frac{a}{\frac{cd+b}{c}}$$

- Then multiply the top of the fraction by the "flip" of the bottom, like so:

$$\frac{a}{\frac{cd+b}{c}} \to \frac{a}{1}\cdot\frac{c}{cd+b} \to \frac{ac}{cd+b}$$

(13) Properties of Numerators and Denominators – There are two properties inherent to the numerators and denominators of every POSITIVE fraction.

- These properties are as follows:

1. **Increasing the numerator makes a fraction bigger, while increasing the denominator makes a fraction smaller.**

   Increasing Numerator: $\frac{1}{5} = 0.2, \frac{2}{5} = 0.4, \frac{3}{5} = 0.6, \frac{4}{5} = 0.8, \frac{5}{5} = 1$

   Increasing Denominator: $\frac{1}{1} = 1, \frac{1}{2} = 0.5, \frac{1}{3} = 0.\overline{3}, \frac{1}{4} = 0.25, \frac{1}{5} = 0.2$

2. **Increasing the numerator and the denominator by the SAME amount brings the value of a fraction closer to 1.**

- Conversely, decreasing the numerator and the denominator by the same amount moves the value of a fraction away from 1.

   Both increase by one: $\frac{1}{2} = 0.5, \frac{2}{3} = 0.\overline{6}, \frac{3}{4} = 0.75 \dots \frac{999}{1,000} \cong 1.$

   Both decrease by two: $\frac{9}{10} = 0.9, \frac{7}{8} = 0.875, \frac{5}{6} = 0.8\overline{3}, \frac{3}{4} = 0.75, \frac{1}{2} = 0.5.$

- To get a sense of how an understanding of these properties can help you, consider the following:

As x increases from 121 to 122, which of the following must increase?

Select all that apply.

$\boxed{A}$ $\frac{2x}{5}$ $\boxed{B}$ $\frac{4+3x}{5+3x}$ $\boxed{C}$ $\frac{5+x}{4+x}$

Answer: A and B. $\boxed{A}$ must increase. If x increases from 121 to 122, the numerator of the fraction increases, and **increasing the numerator** of a positive fraction increases its value.

- $\boxed{B}$ must increase and $\boxed{C}$ must decrease. In both cases, increasing the value of x increases the numerator and denominator **by the same amount**, so the value of each fraction grows **closer to 1**.

- In $\boxed{B}$, the numerator is smaller than the denominator, so its value is **less than 1**. Thus, the fraction **increases** as its value grows closer to 1. In $\boxed{C}$, however, the numerator is larger than the denominator, so its value is **larger than 1**. Thus, the fraction **decreases** as its value grows closer to 1.

Practice Questions

(14) Problem Sets – The following questions have been arranged into three groups: fundamental, intermediate, and rare or advanced.

• Whether you're aiming for a perfect score or a score closer to average, mastery of the concepts in the FUNDAMENTAL questions is absolutely essential.

➢ As you might expect, the INTERMEDIATE questions are more difficult but are essential for test-takers who need an above-average score or higher.

• Finally, the RARE or ADVANCED questions test concepts that are very sophisticated or seldom encountered on the GRE. Mastery of such questions is required only if you need a math score above the 90th percentile.

• As always, if you find yourself confused, bogged down with busy work, or stuck, don't be afraid to fall back on your "Plan B" strategies!

➢ Remember, the "right way" to solve a problem is not always the fastest way, or the smartest.

Fundamental

$$n = \frac{1}{2} + \frac{1}{4} + \frac{1}{8} + \frac{1}{16}$$

Quantity A	Quantity B
1. $1 - n$	$\frac{3}{16}$

2. The value of $\left(1 - \frac{5}{7}\right)\left(1 + \frac{3}{4}\right)$ is

(A) $\frac{1}{28}$ (B) $\frac{3}{14}$ (C) $\frac{9}{28}$ (D) $\frac{13}{28}$ (E) $\frac{1}{2}$

Quantity A	Quantity B
3. $\frac{8}{9} + \frac{1}{81}$	$1 - \frac{1}{27}$

Chapter 4: Fractions

	Quantity A	Quantity B
4.	$\left(3\frac{1}{2}\times1\frac{1}{4}\right)\left(1\frac{5}{7}\div\frac{5}{2}\right)$	$\left(2+\frac{4}{5}\right)-\left(3+\frac{4}{7}\right)$

5. $\dfrac{\frac{2}{2}}{3}+\dfrac{\frac{3}{3}}{4}+\dfrac{\frac{4}{4}}{5}=$

   (A) $\frac{1}{12}$ (B) $\frac{47}{60}$ (C) $\frac{97}{60}$ (D) 11 (E) 12

	Quantity A	Quantity B
6.	$\dfrac{\frac{4}{7}}{\frac{12}{21}}$	$\dfrac{\frac{8}{3}}{\frac{16}{9}}$

7. Which of the following is greater than $\frac{2}{3}$?

   (A) $\frac{33}{50}$ (B) $\frac{8}{11}$ (C) $\frac{3}{5}$ (D) $\frac{13}{27}$ (E) $\frac{5}{8}$

	Quantity A	Quantity B
8.	$\dfrac{4\cdot4\cdot4}{6\cdot6\cdot6}$	$\left(\dfrac{2}{3}\right)^{3}$

9. $2+\left[\left(\dfrac{2}{3}\times\dfrac{3}{8}\right)\div4\right]-\dfrac{9}{16}=$

   (A) $\frac{3}{2}$ (B) $\frac{4}{3}$ (C) $\frac{15}{16}$ (D) $\frac{9}{13}$ (E) 0

10. $\dfrac{14x}{7+x}=$

(A) 1

(B) $\frac{7}{4}$

(C) $\frac{15}{8}$

(D) 2

(E) It cannot be determined from the given information

Intermediate

11. $$\dfrac{\frac{2}{7} \times 21 \times \frac{2}{3} \times 9}{\frac{1}{7} \times 42 \times \frac{1}{3} \times 18} =$$

(A) 2   (B) 1   (C) $\frac{1}{2}$ (D) $\frac{1}{3}$ (E) $\frac{1}{4}$

Quantity A	Quantity B

12. $$\dfrac{1}{5 + \dfrac{1}{4 + \frac{1}{3}}}$$ $$\dfrac{1}{3 + \dfrac{1}{4 + \frac{1}{2}}}$$

13. If $x \neq 0$, then $\dfrac{x+6}{6x} - \dfrac{1}{x} =$

(A) $\dfrac{x+5}{5x}$ (B) $\dfrac{x+5}{6x}$ (C) $\dfrac{-5x+6}{6x}$ (D) $\dfrac{1}{6}$ (E) $-\dfrac{1}{6}$

14. If $\dfrac{x-3}{y+2} = 0$, which of the following must be true?

(A) $x = 3$ and $y = -2$
(B) $x \neq 3$ and $y \neq -2$
(C) $x = 0$ and $y = 0$
(D) $x = 3$ and $y \neq -2$
(E) $x \neq 3$ and $y = -2$

15. The sum of $\frac{6}{7}$ and $\frac{1}{8}$ is between which of the following values?

(A) $\frac{3}{4}$ and $\frac{4}{5}$ (B) $\frac{4}{5}$ and 1   (C) 1 and $\frac{5}{4}$ (D) $\frac{5}{4}$ and $1\frac{1}{2}$ (E) $1\frac{1}{2}$ and 2

Quantity A	Quantity B

16. $$\dfrac{22^3 + 22^2}{22^2}$$ 23

17. If $\frac{a}{b} = \frac{2}{3}$, what is the value of $\frac{a+b}{b}$?

(A) 1

(B) $1\frac{1}{5}$

(C) $1\frac{2}{3}$

(D) $2\frac{1}{3}$

(E) It cannot be determined from the given information

In the fraction $\frac{x}{y}$, where x and y are positive integers, the least common denominator of $\frac{x}{y}$ and $\frac{1}{5}$ is 10.

18.
Quantity A	Quantity B
y	2

19. If $rs \neq 0$, then $\frac{r-1}{rs} =$

(A) $\frac{1}{r} - \frac{1}{rs}$ (B) $\frac{r}{s} - \frac{1}{rs}$ (C) $\frac{1}{s} - r$ (D) $\frac{1}{s} - \frac{1}{rs}$ (E) $\frac{1}{rs} - \frac{1}{s}$

20. In which of the following pairs are the two numbers reciprocals of one other?

Select all possible pairs.

$\boxed{A}$ $\frac{1}{15}$ and 15 $\boxed{B}$ $\frac{1}{11}$ and -11 $\boxed{C}$ $\sqrt{5}$ and $\frac{\sqrt{5}}{5}$

21. Which of the following cannot be a value of $\frac{10}{x+2}$?

(A) -10 (B) -5 (C) -2 (D) 0 (E) 10

At a certain restaurant, Alice paid $\frac{1}{6}$ of the bill, Brenda paid $\frac{1}{5}$ of the bill, Carrie paid $\frac{1}{2}$ more than Brenda, and Darla paid the rest.

Quantity A	Quantity B
	$\frac{1}{2}$

22. The fraction of the bill that Darla paid

Rare or Advanced

23. If $0 < x < 1 < y$, which of the following is true about the reciprocals of x and y?

(A) $1 < \frac{1}{x} < \frac{1}{y}$ (B) $\frac{1}{x} < 1 < \frac{1}{y}$ (C) $\frac{1}{x} < \frac{1}{y} < 1$ (D) $\frac{1}{y} < 1 < \frac{1}{x}$ (E) $\frac{1}{y} < \frac{1}{x} < 1$

$$a - \frac{1}{b} \neq 0$$

Quantity A	Quantity B
24. The reciprocal of $a - \frac{1}{b}$	$\frac{b}{ab - 1}$

25. If $n = -\frac{3}{7}$, which of the following is true?

(A) $n^3 < n^4 < n^2$ (B) $n^3 < n^2 < n^4$ (C) $n^2 < n^4 < n^3$ (D) $n^2 < n^3 < n^4$ (E) $n^4 < n^3 < n^2$

Equal amounts of water are poured into two empty bottles of different capacities, making one bottle $\frac{1}{3}$ full and the other bottle $\frac{1}{2}$ full. The contents of the bottle with the lesser capacity are then poured into the bottle with the greater capacity.

Quantity A	Quantity B
26. The fraction to which the larger bottle is filled with water	$\frac{8}{11}$

27. If x is decreased from 379 to 378, which of the following also decrease?

Select all that apply.

A $\frac{2x}{5}$ B $\frac{4 + 3x}{5 + 3x}$ C $\frac{5 + x}{4 + x}$

28. The expression $\dfrac{\frac{1}{n}}{1 - \frac{1}{n}}$, where $n \neq 0$ or 1, is equivalent to which of the following?

(A) $\frac{1}{n - 1}$ (B) $\frac{1}{1 - n}$ (C) $1 - n$ (D) $\frac{n}{n - 1}$ (E) $\frac{n}{1 - n}$

(15) Solutions – Video solutions for each of the previous questions can be found on our website at **www.sherpaprep.com/videos**.

• BOOKMARK this address for future visits!

> ➤ To view the videos, you'll need the LOGIN and PASSWORD that you created upon registering your copy of <u>Arithmetic & "Plan B" Strategies</u>.

• If you have yet to register your book yet, please go to **www.sherpaprep.com/activate** and enter your email address, last name, and shipping address.

• Be sure to provide the SAME last name and shipping address that you used to purchase your copy of <u>Master Key to the GRE</u> or to enroll in your GRE course with Sherpa Prep!

> ➤ When checking your answers, we encourage you to watch the solution for any problem that you answered INCORRECTLY

• The same goes for any problem that took you MORE than TWO MINUTES to solve.

• After digesting the explanation, REVISIT your mistake a couple of days later to ensure that the problem no longer poses issues to you.

> ➤ If you struggle to solve the problem a SECOND time, add it to your "LOG of ERRORS" and redo it every few weeks.

• Solving tricky questions MORE THAN ONCE is the best way to learn from your mistakes and to avoid similar difficulties on your actual exam.

Fundamental	Intermediate		Rare or Advanced
1. B	11. B	21. D	23. D
2. E	12. B	22. B	24. C
3. B	13. D		25. A
4. A	14. D		26. B
5. E	15. B		27. A, B
6. B	16. C		28. A
7. B	17. C		
8. C	18. D		
9. A	19. D		
10. E	20. A, C		

Chapter 5

Decimals

Decimals

To be discussed:

Fundamental Concepts

Whether you're aiming for a perfect score or a score closer to average, mastery of the following concepts is essential.

Rare or Advanced Concepts

The following concepts are either advanced or are tested only on rare occasions. If you don't need an elite math score, don't waste your time!

Practice Questions

There's no substitute for elbow grease. Practice your new skills to ensure that you internalize what you've studied.

Fundamental Concepts

(1) Introduction – Like fractions, decimals are an important part of the revised GRE.

• Although relatively few questions involve decimals exclusively, many questions require the ability to work with decimals quickly and easily.

 ➢ What's more, **most of these questions cannot be solved with the GRE calculator.**

• And this should be expected. Remember, exam-makers are not interested in your ability to use a calculator. They're interested in your ability to find smart, simple solutions to problems that seem complex or time-consuming.

• As such, it's unlikely that they'll give you a problem that's as simple as mindlessly plugging numbers into a calculator.

 ➢ To prepare yourself properly for GRE decimal questions, you'll need a solid understanding of several properties and concepts.

• You'll also need to know a few techniques to make manipulating decimals easy.

• Before we introduce them to you, however, let's make sure that you're familiar with some basic information about decimals.

 ➢ As you may know, **each position in a decimal is associated with a particular place value.**

• These place values are as follows:

$$\overset{\text{Thousands Hundreds Tens Units Tenths Hundredths Thousandths}}{8,213.654}$$

> ➤ Any number in the **thousands** column represents that number × **1,000**.

• Likewise, any number in the hundreds column represents that number × 100, any number in the tens column represents that number × 10, and any number in the units column represents that number × 1.

• For example, in the number 8,213.654:

$$8 = 8 \times 1,000 \qquad 2 = 2 \times 100 \qquad 1 = 1 \times 10 \qquad 3 = 3 \times 1$$

> ➤ Similarly, any number in the **tenths** column represents that number ÷ **10**.

• Likewise, any number in the hundredths column represents that number ÷ 100, and any number in the thousandths column represents that number ÷ 1,000.

• For example, in the number 8,213.654:

$$6 = \frac{6}{10} = 0.6 \qquad 5 = \frac{5}{100} = 0.05 \qquad 4 = \frac{4}{1,000} = 0.004$$

> ➤ Each number in a decimal is known as a **digit**, and there are 10 digits: 0, 1, 2, 3, 4, 5, 6, 7, 8, and 9.

1.07 has three digits: 1, 0, 7
218.43 has five digits: 2, 1, 8, 4, 3

• Whole numbers, which are technically known as **integers**, are sometimes described by the number of digits they hold:

23 is a "two-digit integer"
8,007 is a "four-digit integer"

• Unlike integers, however, decimals are never described this way, since the number of digits in any decimal can always be increased by adding superfluous zeroes to its end:

$$4.2 = 4.20 = 4.200$$

• Finally, any integer can be written as a decimal by affixing a decimal point and a zero to its end:

$$6 = 6.0 \qquad 15 = 15.0 \qquad 217 = 217.0$$

(2) Rounding Decimals – Limiting the value of a decimal to a specified place value is known as rounding.

- To round decimals, find the specified place value, or "rounding digit", and look at the digit **immediately to its right**:

> ➤ If the digit to the right is less than 5, **leave the "rounding digit" unchanged** and drop all the digits to its right.

- If the digit to the right is 5 or greater, **add one to the "rounding digit"** and drop all of the digits to its right.

- Let's take a look at two rounding problems, the first of which is relatively straightforward and the second a bit trickier.

What is 25.316 rounded to the nearest hundredth?

(A) 25   (B) 25.3   (C) 25.31   (D) 25.317   (E) 25.32

Answer: E. To round 25.316 to the nearest hundredth, we first must find its "rounding digit". Since a **1 is located in the hundredths column**, the "rounding digit" is 1.

> ➤ If we look one digit to the right of the "rounding digit", we see a 6. Since 6 is greater than 5, we must add one to the "rounding digit" and drop all digits to its right.

- Thus, the correct answer is (E), since 25.316 rounded to the nearest hundredth is 25.32.

If 1.2*n*5 is rounded to the nearest tenth, which of the following could be the tenths digit of the rounded number?

(A) 1   (B) 2   (C) 4   (D) 5   (E) 6

Answer: B. According to the problem, 1.2*n*5 is to be rounded to the nearest tenth. Since a **2 is located in the tenths column**, the "rounding digit" is 2. If we look one digit to the right of the "rounding digit", we see the digit *n*.

> ➤ Although we do not know the value of *n*, we know that we must add one to the "rounding digit" if *n* is 5 or greater and leave it unchanged if *n* is less than 5.

- Thus, if *n* is 5 or greater, the tenths digit must be rounded to 3. Likewise, if *n* is less than 5, the tenths digit must remain as 2. Since 3 is NOT given as an answer choice, the tenths digit of the rounded number can ONLY be 2. The correct answer is therefore (B).

(3) Powers of Ten – Any number formed by multiplying one or more tens together is known as a "power of ten".

- For example, numbers such as 10, 100, and 10^4 would all be considered powers of ten, since $10 = 10 \times 1$, $100 = 10 \times 10$, and $10^4 = 10 \times 10 \times 10 \times 10$.

- Likewise, numbers such as 3 and 20 would not, since neither 3 nor 20 consists solely of "10"s. Thus, $3 = 3 \times 1$ and $20 = 2 \times 10$.

> **Multiplying a number by a power of ten** slides the decimal point of that number to the <u>right</u>, since multiplying by a number greater than 1 makes a number larger.

- The number of slides to the <u>right</u> will equal the number of zeroes in the power of ten:

$0.107 \times 100 = 10.7$ "2 zeroes" → slide the decimal 2 places to the right.
$0.123 \times 1{,}000 = 123$ "3 zeroes" → slide the decimal 3 places to the right.

- If the power of ten is written in the form 10^n, **the number of slides will equal the exponent n:**

$5.71 \times 10^3 = 5{,}710$ 10^3 → slide the decimal 3 places to the right.
$0.021 \times 10^6 = 21{,}000$ 10^6 → slide the decimal 6 places to the right.

> **Dividing a number by a power of ten** slides the decimal point of that number to the <u>left</u>, since dividing by a number greater than 1 makes a number smaller.

- The number of slides to the <u>left</u> will equal the number of zeroes in the power of ten:

$0.123 \div 100 = 0.00123$ "2 zeroes" → slide the decimal 2 places to the left.
$17 \div 1{,}000 = 0.017$ "3 zeroes" → slide the decimal 3 places to the left.

- If the power of ten is written in the form 10^n, **the number of slides will equal the exponent n:**

$5.71 \div 10^3 = 0.00571$ 10^3 → slide the decimal 3 places to the left.
$21 \div 10^6 = 0.000021$ 10^6 → slide the decimal 6 places to the left.

> When sliding decimal points, be sure to **add zeroes** if you need to:

$5.71 \times 10^4 = 57{,}100$ 10^4 → add 2 zeroes to the right of 5.71.
$2.13 \div 10^4 = 0.000213$ 10^4 → add 3 zeroes to the left of 2.13.

➢ **Powers of ten written in the form 10^{-n}** work in the **opposite direction** of regular powers of ten.

• Multiplying by 10^{-n} will slide the decimal point to the left, and dividing by 10^{-n} will slide the decimal point to the right. For example:

$$5.71 \times 10^{-3} = 0.00571 \qquad 10^{-3} \rightarrow 3 \text{ slides in the opposite direction of } 10^{3}.$$
$$2.14 \div 10^{-6} = 2,140,000 \qquad 10^{-6} \rightarrow 6 \text{ slides in the opposite direction of } 10^{6}.$$

• Now that we've covered the principal ideas, let's take a look at a couple of typical GRE problems involving powers of ten:

Quantity A	**Quantity B**
$\dfrac{0.004 \div 10^{-3}}{0.012 \div 10^{-4}}$	$\dfrac{1}{30}$

Answer. C. Dividing a number by 10^{n} slides its decimal point n places to the <u>left</u>. However, powers of ten **in the form 10^{-n}** work in the **opposite manner** of regular powers of ten. Thus, dividing a number 10^{-n} slides its decimal point n spaces to the <u>right</u>:

$$\frac{0.004 \div 10^{-3}}{0.012 \div 10^{-4}} \quad \rightarrow \quad \frac{4 \ (3 \text{ slides})}{120 \ (4 \text{ slides})}$$

• Since $\dfrac{4}{120} = \dfrac{\cancel{4}(1)}{\cancel{4}(30)} = \dfrac{1}{30}$, the two quantities are equal.

$2,135 \times 10^{n}$ equals a number between 1 and 10

Quantity A	**Quantity B**
The value of integer n	-3

Answer. C. The decimal equivalent of 2,135 is 2,135.0. If we slide the decimal point of 2,135.0 three places to the left, we get 2.135: a number bigger than 1 but less than 10.

$$2,135.0 \ \rightarrow \ 2.135 \ (3 \text{ slides left})$$

• According to the problem, n must be an integer (whole number). If $n = -2$, the decimal point would slide 2 spaces to the left, giving us 21.35: a number bigger than 10. If $n = -4$, the decimal point would slide 4 spaces to the left, giving us 0.2135: a number less than 1.

• If $n = -3$, the decimal point would slide 3 spaces to the left, giving us 2.135: a number between 1 and 10. Since n must be a whole number, the two quantities have to be equal.

(4) Addition and Subtraction – Adding and subtracting decimals is a relatively insignificant aspect of GRE math.

• Very few questions test this concept directly, since most decimals can be added with a calculator. That said, questions sometimes require the addition of decimals as a step towards the correct answer, so you want to be able to do so quickly.

> ➤ To add or subtract decimals, write down the numbers, one under the other, **with the decimal points lined up**.

• Once you've done this, **insert zeros so the numbers have the same length** and then add (or subtract) the columns. Don't forget to put the decimal point in your answer!

• On the left, let's add 1.452, 2.12, and 1.3. On the right, let's subtract 8 and 0.075:

$$
\begin{array}{ll}
\quad 1.452 & \\
\quad 2.120 & \text{add 1 zero} \\
+ \ 1.300 & \text{add 2 zeroes} \\
\hline
\quad 4.872 &
\end{array}
\qquad\qquad
\begin{array}{ll}
\quad 8.000 & \text{add 3 zeroes} \\
- \ 0.075 & \\
\hline
\quad 7.925 &
\end{array}
$$

> ➤ From time to time, exam-makers will design questions about adding and subtracting decimals. These questions almost always involve **mystery digits**.

• Such problems can easily be solved by substituting a variable such as x for the number with the mystery digits. Consider the following:

$$
\begin{array}{r}
138.3 \\
- \ \nabla \Diamond . \Delta \\
\hline
68.5
\end{array}
$$

In the correctly performed subtraction shown above,
∇, $\Diamond$, and Δ represent digits between 0 and 9, inclusive.

Quantity A	**Quantity B**
$\Diamond + \Delta$	17

Answer: C. Although the mystery digits ∇, $\Diamond$, and Δ make this problem look intimidating, we can easily solve it by substituting the variable x for those digits:

$$138.3 - x = 68.5$$

➢ As we will show you in the Algebra chapter of our book on <u>Number Properties & Algebra</u>, the value of x is easy to determine in an equation like this.

• To do so, first add x to both sides of the equation:

$$138.3 - x = 68.5$$
$$138.3 = 68.5 + x \qquad \text{Add } x \text{ to both sides.}$$

• Then, subtract 68.5 from both sides:

$$138.3 = 68.5 + x$$
$$138.3 - 68.5 = x \qquad \text{Subtract 68.5 from both sides.}$$

➢ If you feel as though a calculation like $138.3 - 68.5$ would be difficult to do by hand, feel free to let the calculator do the work.

• Thus, we know that $x = 69.8$, since $138.3 - 68.5 = 69.8$. Likewise, we also know the following, since x represents the mystery digits $\nabla\Diamond.\Delta$:

$$\nabla\Diamond.\Delta = 69.8$$

• From this, we can see that the mystery digit $\nabla = 6$, the mystery digit $\Diamond = 9$, and the mystery digit $\Delta = 8$. Thus, Quantities A and B must be equal, since $\Diamond + \Delta = 9 + 8 = 17$. The correct answer is, therefore, (C).

(5) Converting Decimals to Fractions – There are several ways to convert a decimal to a fraction.

• The easiest way is a two-step process. First, **place the digits of your decimal over a 1**. Then, beside that 1, insert zeroes.

> ➤ The number of zeroes should **equal the number of decimal places** in the decimal.

• For example, the decimal 0.123 contains 3 decimal places, so its digits should be placed over 3 zeroes. Similarly, the decimal 0.37 contains 2 decimal places, so its digits should be placed over 2 zeroes:

$$0.123 = \frac{123}{1,000} \qquad\qquad 0.37 = \frac{37}{100}$$

• Be sure to simplify the resulting fraction, if necessary:

$$0.0625 = \frac{625}{10,000} = \frac{25(25)}{100(100)} = \frac{1(1)}{4(4)} = \frac{1}{16}$$

> ➤ Conversely, if you need to convert **a decimal into a fraction**, the easiest way to do so is with our "Conversion List".

• As you may recall from our discussion of Arithmetic, the "Conversion List" is a small table of fractions and their decimal equivalents:

$$\frac{1}{2} = 0.5 \qquad \frac{1}{5} = 0.2 \qquad \frac{1}{8} = 0.125 \qquad \frac{1}{11} = 0.\overline{09}$$

$$\frac{1}{3} = 0.\overline{3} \qquad \frac{1}{6} = 0.1\overline{6} \qquad \frac{1}{9} = 0.\overline{1} \qquad \frac{1}{99} = 0.\overline{01}$$

$$\frac{1}{4} = 0.25 \qquad \frac{1}{7} \approx 0.14 \qquad \frac{1}{10} = 0.1 \qquad \frac{1}{100} = 0.01$$

• Knowing this chart will allow you to convert most fractions into decimals quickly and easily. For example, if you know that $\frac{1}{8} = 0.125,$ then you can deduce that $\frac{3}{8} = 0.375$ and $\frac{5}{8} = 0.625$, since:

$$\frac{3}{8} = 3 \times \frac{1}{8} = 3 \times 0.125 = 0.375 \qquad\qquad \frac{5}{8} = \frac{4}{8} + \frac{1}{8} = 0.5 + 0.125 = 0.625$$

• Likewise, if you know that $\frac{1}{7} \approx 0.14,$ then you can deduce that $\frac{2}{7} \approx 0.28$ and $\frac{6}{7} \approx 0.86$, as:

$$\frac{2}{7} = 2 \times \frac{1}{7} = 2 \times 0.14 \approx 0.28 \qquad\qquad \frac{6}{7} = \frac{7}{7} - \frac{1}{7} = 1 - 0.14 \approx 0.86$$

➤ On rare occasions, you may come across a fraction whose denominator is not part of our "Conversion List".

- If the list isn't helpful for a particular fraction, simply **set the bottom of that fraction equal to a power of ten**, such as 100 or 1,000.

- And remember: whatever you do to the bottom of a fraction, you also need to do to the top. Thus, $\frac{7}{20} = 0.35$ and $\frac{8}{25} = 0.32$, since:

$$\frac{7}{20} = \frac{7(5)}{20(5)} = \frac{35}{100} = 0.35 \qquad\qquad \frac{8}{25} = \frac{8(4)}{25(4)} = \frac{32}{100} = 0.32$$

➤ Visually, you can think of this technique as follows:

$$\times 2$$
$$\frac{17}{50} = \frac{34}{100} = 0.34$$
$$\times 2$$

- Let's take a look at a sample GRE problem involving conversions:

$$\frac{3}{4}, \frac{18}{25}, \frac{7}{10}, \frac{5}{8}$$

.75   .72 .7 .125
                .625

Quantity A	**Quantity B**
The greatest of the four fractions given above	The sum of 0.125 and the least of the four fractions given above

C

Answer. C. To solve this problem, we first need to determine the greatest and least of these fractions. We can do so by using the conversion techniques discussed above to ascertain their decimal values:

$$\frac{3}{4} = 3 \times \frac{1}{4} = 3 \times 0.25 = \boxed{0.75} \qquad\qquad \frac{18}{25} = \frac{18(4)}{25(4)} = \frac{72}{100} = \boxed{0.72}$$

$$\frac{7}{10} = 7 \times \frac{1}{10} = 7 \times 0.1 = \boxed{0.7} \qquad\qquad \frac{5}{8} = \frac{4}{8} + \frac{1}{8} = 0.5 + 0.125 = \boxed{0.625}$$

- Since 0.75 is the greatest of these values, Quantity A = 0.75. Conversely, since 0.625 is the least of the values, Quantity B = 0.125 + 0.625. Thus, the quantities must be equal, since 0.125 + 0.625 = 0.750 = 0.75. The correct answer is, therefore, (C).

(6) Multiplication and Division – As discussed, the addition and subtraction of decimals is a relatively insignificant aspect of GRE math.

• The same cannot be said for the multiplication and division of decimals. You'll encounter these operations more frequently, so it's important that you be able to perform them quickly.

➢ To multiply decimals, first **ignore the decimals**. Multiply the numbers as if they were whole numbers.

• Then, **add up the number of decimal places** in the question. The question and the answer should have the same number of decimal places.

• For example, imagine that you needed to multiply 0.03×1.1 or 0.002×0.08:

$$
\begin{array}{rl}
0.03 & \text{2 decimal places} \\
\times\ 1.1 & +\ \text{1 decimal place} \\
\hline
0.033 & \text{3 decimal places}
\end{array}
\qquad
\begin{array}{rl}
0.002 & \text{3 decimal places} \\
\times\ 0.08 & +\ \text{2 decimal places} \\
\hline
0.00016 & \text{5 decimal places}
\end{array}
$$

• In the case of 0.03×1.1, if we multiply the numbers without their decimals, we get $3 \times 11 = 33$. But since 0.03 has **2 decimal places** and 1.1 has **1 decimal place**, the answer must have **3 decimal places**, giving us 0.033.

➢ To divide decimals, first **put the division in fraction form**.

• Then **"slide" away the decimal points until they're gone**. Be sure to slide each decimal point an <u>equal</u> number of times. (<u>Remember</u>, whatever you do to the bottom of a fraction <u>must</u> be done to the top!)

• For example, imagine that you needed to divide $35 \div 1.4$ or $0.5 \div 0.08$:

$$
\frac{35}{1.4} = \frac{350 \ (\text{1 slide})}{14 \ (\text{1 slide})} = \frac{7(50)}{7(2)} = 25
\qquad
\frac{0.5}{0.08} = \frac{50 \ (\text{2 slides})}{8 \ (\text{2 slides})} = \frac{2(25)}{2(4)} = 6\frac{1}{4} = 6.25
$$

• Notice that once we slide each decimal an <u>equal</u> number of places on the top and bottom, the resulting fractions are easy to break down since they **no longer contain decimals**.

➢ If the decimal equivalent of your fraction isn't obvious, simply convert it with one of our conversion techniques discussed earlier. For example, $0.02 \div 0.4 = 0.05$, since:

$$
\frac{0.02}{0.4} = \frac{2 \ (\text{2 slides})}{40 \ (\text{2 slides})} = \frac{1}{20} \ \rightarrow \ \frac{1(5)}{20(5)} = \frac{5}{100} = 0.05
$$

➢ From time to time, exam-makers will design questions about multiplying and dividing decimals that involve **mystery digits**, such as the one below.

• In general, the key to solving such problems is to remember that multiplication and division are opposite operations. If $21 \div 3 = 7$, then $3 \times 7 = 21$. Likewise, if $4 \times 8 = 32$, then $32 \div 8 = 4$.

• Consider the following:

$$
\begin{array}{r}
7 \\
62.4\overline{)\,437.\square} \\
-436.\triangle \\
\hline
0.3
\end{array}
$$

If the solution of the division problem above is correct, what digit does □ represent?

(A) 6 (B) 4 (C) 2 (D) 1 (E) 0

Answer: D. According to the division above, 62.4 goes into "437. □" **seven times**, with 0.3 left over. Since division and multiplication are opposite operations, 62.4×7 must therefore equal a number slightly less than "437. □". Specifically, that number must be 436.8, as:

$$62.4 \times 7 = 436.8 \quad \longleftarrow \quad \text{Use the calculator}$$

➢ From this, we can deduce that the $\triangle = 8$, since the second line of the long division indicates that "436. $\triangle$" = 436.8.

• And if "436. $\triangle$" = 436.8, then we know that:

$$
\begin{array}{r}
437.\square \\
-436.\,8 \\
\hline
0.\,3
\end{array}
$$

• Like other mystery digit problems that involve addition or subtraction, we can easily determine the value of the mystery digit by replacing "437. □" with an x.

➢ Doing so gives us:

$$x - 436.8 = 0.3$$

• By adding 436.8 to both sides of the equation, we learn that $x = 437.1$. As such, the □ must equal 1, since x also equals "437. □". Thus, the answer is (D).

(7) Decimals Between 0 and 1 – Like fractions, decimals between 0 and 1 have SPECIAL properties.

- These properties can be summarized as follows:

  ➤ When MULTIPLIED with or DIVIDED against positive values, decimals between 0 and 1 produce the OPPOSITE results of numbers <u>larger</u> than 1. For example:

- ▢**Multiplying** a positive value by a number larger than 1 makes the value bigger. Multiplying a positive value by a decimal between 0 and 1, however, makes that value smaller.

$$\text{Larger than 1: } \boxed{10} \times 2 \rightarrow \boxed{20} \qquad \text{Between 0 and 1: } \boxed{10} \times (0.5) \rightarrow \boxed{5}$$

- ▢**Dividing** a positive value by a number larger than 1 makes that value smaller. Dividing a positive value by a decimal between 0 and 1, however, makes that value bigger.

$$\text{Larger than 1: } \boxed{10} \div 2 \rightarrow \boxed{5} \qquad \text{Between 0 and 1: } \boxed{10} \div (0.5) \rightarrow \boxed{20}$$

  ➤ Likewise, the SQUARES and SQUARE ROOTS of decimals between 0 and 1 also behave in the OPPOSITE manner of other <u>positive</u> squares and square roots:

- ▢**Squaring** a positive value larger than 1 makes that value bigger. Squaring a decimal between 0 and 1, however, makes that decimal smaller.

$$\text{Larger than 1: } 10^2 \rightarrow \boxed{100} \qquad \text{Between 0 and 1: } \left(0.5\right)^2 \rightarrow \boxed{0.25}$$

- ▢**Taking the Square Root** of a positive value larger than 1 makes that value smaller. Taking the square root of a decimal between 0 and 1, however, makes that decimal bigger.

$$\text{Larger than 1: } \sqrt{4} \rightarrow \boxed{2} \qquad \text{Between 0 and 1: } \sqrt{0.5} \rightarrow \boxed{\cong 0.71}$$

  ➤ Many questions test this concept specifically.

- The difficulty of such questions can be GREATLY reduced if you RECOGNIZE the concept rather than compute the numbers.

- Consider the following:

Quantity A	**Quantity B**
$\sqrt{0.9} + \sqrt[3]{0.9} + \sqrt[4]{0.9}$	$(0.9)^2 + (0.9)^3 + (0.9)^4$

Answer: A. Although we might be tempted to solve this problem by calculator, doing so would not only be time-consuming but also fruitless: the GRE calculator is awkward to use and cannot compute cube roots, fourth roots, or exponents.

➤ To solve this problem, we simply need to recognize that **squaring a decimal between 0 and 1 makes the original number smaller.**

- Thus, $(0.9)^2$ gets smaller when we square it: $(0.9)^2 = 0.9 \times 0.9 = 0.81$.

- The same is also true of $(0.9)^3$ and $(0.9)^4$, since the more we multiply by a decimal between 0 and 1, the smaller the original number gets.

➤ Conversely, **the taking the root of a decimal between 0 and 1 makes the original number bigger**.

- Hence, the square root of 0.9 is bigger than 0.9: $\sqrt{0.9} \approx 0.95$. (If you can't compute this by hand, don't worry: even we had to use a calculator!)

- The same is also true of $\sqrt[3]{0.9}$ and $\sqrt[4]{0.9}$, since the higher the root we take of a decimal between 0 and 1, the bigger the original number gets.

➤ Therefore, $\sqrt{0.9} + \sqrt[3]{0.9} + \sqrt[4]{0.9}$ **is the addition of three numbers bigger than 0.9**, while $(0.9)^2 + (0.9)^3 + (0.9)^4$ is the addition of three numbers smaller than 0.9.

- Because Quantity A is larger than Quantity B, the correct answer must be (A).

(8) Units Digits – From time to time, exam-makers will design questions that require you to determine the units digit (aka the "ones digit") of a very large product or sum.

- At first glance, such questions can be very intimidating, since the numbers involved are typically enormous and way too large to calculate.

- Fortunately, despite their appearance, such problems are very easy to solve.

  ➤ To determine the units (ones) digit of a product or sum of integers (whole numbers), you simply need to remember one thing: **only the units digits matter**.

- **The other digits are irrelevant** and can be dropped before you multiply or add.

- For example, the units digit of the product of 783×476 would be 8, while the units digit of $4{,}329 + 165$ would be 4:

783×476	3 and 6 are the units digits.	$4{,}329 + 165$	9 and 5 are the units digits.
3×6	Drop the other digits.	$9 + 5$	Drop the other digits.
$3 \times 6 = 1\boxed{8}$	The units digit is 8.	$9 + 5 = 1\boxed{4}$	The units digit is 4.

- To get a better sense of why this is so, let's take a closer look at the multiplication of 783×476 and the addition of $4{,}329 + 165$.

- If we multiply 783×476 by hand, we see that **the units digit of the product** is the result of 3×6, the units digits of 783 and 476. And if we add $4{,}329 + 165$, we likewise see that **the units digit of the sum** is the result of $9 + 5$, the units digits of 4,329 and 165:

$$
\begin{array}{r}
783 \\
\times\ \ 476 \\
\hline
4{,}698 \\
\dots 10 \\
+\ \ \dots 200 \\
\hline
\dots 0\boxed{8}
\end{array}
\qquad
\begin{array}{r}
4{,}329 \\
+\ \ \ \ 165 \\
\hline
\dots 9\boxed{4}
\end{array}
$$

  ➤ On rare occasions, exam-makers may ask you about the **tens digit** of a large product or sum.

- As can be seen from the multiplication and addition problems above, **the tens digit of a product or sum depends on the units <u>and</u> tens digits** of the integers involved. The other digits are irrelevant.

> ➤ Thus, if you need to get the tens digits of some product or sum, you simply need to remember one thing: **only the units and tens digits matter.**

• <u>DROP</u> the other digits before multiplying or adding. Let's take a look at a couple of typical GRE problems involving units digits:

Which of the following equals the units digit of $(23)^3(12)^4(67)^2$?

$7 \quad 6 \quad 9$

(A) 0 (B) 2 (C) 4 (D) 6 (E) 8

Answer. E. Although our calculator can multiply $23 \times 23 \times 23$ or 67×67, it cannot multiply $(23)^3(12)^4(67)^2$, since the product of these three numbers is greater than 99,999,999.

> ➤ We know, however, that $23 \times 23 \times 23$ has a units digit of 7, since the product of the units digits equals $3 \times 3 \times 3 = 2\boxed{7}$.

• Likewise, we know that $12 \times 12 \times 12 \times 12$ and 67×67 have units digits of 6 and 9, respectively, since the products of their units digits equal $2 \times 2 \times 2 \times 2 = 1\boxed{6}$ and $7 \times 7 = 4\boxed{9}$.

• Because the units digits of 23^3, 12^4, and 67^2 are 7, 6, and 9, the product of $(23)^3(12)^4(67)^2$ must have a units digit of 8, since $7 \times 6 \times 9 = 42 \times 9 = 37\boxed{8}$. Thus, the answer is (E).

$$k = 41{,}227 \times 34{,}115$$

Quantity A	**Quantity B**
The units digit of k	**The tens digit of k**

Answer. A. **To get the units digit** of a product or sum, we simply need to drop any digits that are NOT units digits before multiplying or adding. Thus, the units digit of k is 5, since:

$41{,}22\boxed{7} \times 34{,}11\boxed{5}$	1 and 5 are the units digits.
7×5	Drop the other digits.
$7 \times 5 = 3\boxed{5}$	The units digit is 5.

• **To get the tens digit** of a product or sum, we simply need to drop any digits that are NOT units <u>or</u> tens digits before multiplying or adding. Thus, the tens digit of k is 0, since:

$41{,}2\boxed{27} \times 34{,}1\boxed{15}$	27 and 15 are the units/tens digits.
27×15	Drop the other digits.
$27 \times 15 = 4\boxed{0}5$	The tens digit is 0.

• Since 5 is larger than 0, Quantity A is larger than Quantity B. Therefore, the answer is (A).

Chapter 5: Decimals

Rare or Advanced Concepts

(9) Repeating Digits – Every now and them, exam-makers may ask you to **identify a specific term** within a pattern of repeating digits.

• For example, given the repeating decimal 0.345345345…, you might be asked to identify its 41st digit to the right of the decimal point.

> The key to solving such problems is to **remove the completed "cycles" before your digit**.

• Every time a pattern repeats, it completes one "cycle". For example, you can think of each "cycle" in the repeating decimal 0.42384238… as:

$$0.\boxed{4238}\boxed{4328}\boxed{4238}\boxed{4238}\ldots$$

> Imagine that you wanted to know the 22nd digit to the right of the decimal point. If you were to **remove the first 5 "cycles"**, you would remove the first 20 digits:

$$0.\boxed{4238}\boxed{4328}\boxed{4238}\boxed{4238}\boxed{4238}42\ldots \quad \textbf{22}^{\textbf{nd}} \textbf{ digit}$$

• The next two digits would be the 21st and the 22nd. Since each "cycle" begins 4, 2, 3… the 21st digit would be a 4 and the **22nd digit would be a 2**, as can be seen in the visual approach depicted above.

In the repeating decimal 0.0481304813…, the sum of the 32nd and 43rd digits to the right of the decimal point is

(A) 5 (B) 7 (C) 8 (D) 12 (E) 13

Answer. D. The repeating decimal 0.0481304813… repeats every 5 digits: 0, 4, 8, 1, 3.

Before the 32nd term, this "cycle" completes itself 6 times, since each "cycle" has 5 digits. If we were to remove the 30 digits in these 6 "cycles", the next 2 digits would be the 31st and 32nd. Since each "cycle" begins 0, 4, 8,…, the 31st term = 0 and the 32nd term = 4.

Before the 43rd term, the "cycle" completes itself 8 times. If we were to remove the 40 digits in these 8 "cycles", the next 3 digits would be the 41st, 42nd, and 43rd. Since each "cycle" begins 0, 4, 8,…, the 43rd term = 8.

• Thus, the correct answer must be (D), since the sum of the 32nd and 43rd digits equals $4+8=12$.

Sherpa
Prep

➤ Advanced questions about **units digits** often involve patterns of repeating digits.

• Consider the following:

Quantity A	**Quantity B**
The value of the units digit in 2^{33}	The value of the units digit in 3^{22}

Answer. B. Numbers such as 2^{33} and 3^{22} are too large to be multiplied by calculator or by hand. We can, however, determine their units digits by **looking for patterns**.

➤ To start, we know that the first four powers of 2 are $2^1 = 2$, $2^2 = 4$, $2^3 = 8$, and $2^4 = 16$.

• We may not know the value of 2^5, but we know that **2^5 ends in a 2, since $2^4 \times 2 = 16 \times 2$**. Likewise, we may not know the value of 2^6, but we know that 2^6 ends in a 4, since 2^5 ends in a 2 and "this 2" $\times 2 = 4$.

• Thus, we can see that powers of 2 end in the "cycle" 2, 4, 8, 6, since the next four powers of 2 also end in the pattern 2, 4, 8, 6:

	ends in
$2^5 = 2^4 \times 2 = 16 \times 2$	2
$2^6 = 2^5 \times 2 =$ "ends in 2" $\times 2$	4
$2^7 = 2^6 \times 2 =$ "ends in 4" $\times 2$	8
$2^8 = 2^7 \times 2 =$ "ends in 8" $\times 2$	6

➤ To get the **units digit of 2^{33}**, therefore, we simply need to remove the first 8 "cycles", as follows:

2486|2486|2486|2486|2486|2486|2486|2486|2...   **33ʳᵈ term**

• Likewise, the first four powers of 3 are $3^1 = 3$, $3^2 = 9$, $3^3 = 27$, and $3^4 = 81$, so we can see that powers of 3 end in the "cycle" 3, 9, 7, 1, since the next four powers end as follows:

	ends in
$3^5 = 3^4 \times 3 = 81 \times 3$	3
$3^6 = 3^5 \times 3 =$ "ends in 3" $\times 3$	9
$3^7 = 3^6 \times 3 =$ "ends in 9" $\times 3$	7
$3^8 = 3^7 \times 3 =$ "ends in 7" $\times 3$	1

• Thus, to get the **units digit of 3^{22}**, we simply need to remove the first 5 "cycles", as follows:

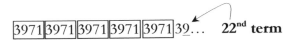

$$\boxed{3971}\boxed{3971}\boxed{3971}\boxed{3971}\boxed{3971}39\ldots \quad \textbf{22}^{\textbf{nd}} \textbf{ term}$$

• As we can see, the units digit of 2^{33} is 2 and that of 3^{22} is 9. The correct answer is therefore (B).

➤ On a final note, it's worth pointing out that **the powers of every number from 1 to 10 end in a pattern**.

• Here they are:

Power	Pattern of the Units Digits
1	Always ends in a 1
2	2, 4, 8, 6
3	3, 9, 7, 1
4	4, 6
5	Always ends in a 5
6	Always ends in a 6
7	7, 9, 3, 1
8	8, 4, 2, 6
9	9, 1
10	Always ends in a 0

➤ It's **not important** that you memorize these patterns. Just be sure that you can tease them out quickly if you need to.

• When doing so, it can be helpful to remember that **no UNITS DIGITS pattern is ever longer than FOUR digits** (as you can see from the table above).

• Thus, if you know the first four powers of a number from 1 to 10, you know the pattern of its units digits! Hence, the first four powers of 4 are $4^1 = \underline{4}$, $4^2 = 1\underline{6}$, $4^3 = 6\underline{4}$, and $4^4 = 25\underline{6}$, so the units digits of powers of 4 end in the pattern 4, 6.

(10) Reversed Digits – On very rare occasions, exam-makers may ask you to add or subtract two mystery numbers whose digits are the same but in reverse order.

• "Reversed digit" questions can seem quite difficult, particularly when "Plan B" strategies such as backsolving are ineffective.

➢ The key to solving such problems is to **represent the numbers algebraically**.

• **Any two-digit integer can be represented as 10x + y**, where 10x = the tens digit and y = the units digit of that integer. Conversely, a different integer with the same digits, but in reverse order, can be represented as 10y + x.

• To prove this, let $x = 2$ and $y = 3$. Inserted into 10x + y, the two-digit integer would be $10(2) + 3 = \boxed{23}$. But inserted into 10y + x, the two-digit integer would have the same digits, but in reverse order: $10(3) + 2 = \boxed{32}$.

➢ When solving reversed digit problems, **be sure to add or subtract the algebraic representations**, as the problem dictates, in order to solve the problem.

• Consider the following:

If the two-digit integers P and Q are positive and have the same digits, but in reverse order, which of the following CANNOT be the sum of P and Q?

(A) 158   (B) 121   (C) 110   (D) 55   (E) 44

Answer. A. Since P and Q have the same digits, but in reverse order, let's first represent each integer algebraically:

$$P = 10x + y \qquad Q = 10y + x$$

➢ Next let's add the two, since the question asks us about **the sum of P and Q**:

$$\begin{array}{r} 10x + y \\ +\ \underline{(10y + x)} \\ 11x + 11y \rightarrow 11(x+y) \end{array}$$

• Since $P + Q = 11(x + y)$, the sum of P and Q must be a multiple of 11. Looking back at our answers, (A) must be correct, since (A) is the only answer choice NOT divisible by 11:

(A) $\dfrac{158}{11} = 14.\overline{36}$ (B) $\dfrac{121}{11} = 11$ (C) $\dfrac{110}{11} = 10$ (D) $\dfrac{55}{11} = 11$ (E) $\dfrac{44}{11} = 4$

> ➤ **A three-digit integer can be represented as $100x + 10y + z$**, where $100x =$ the <u>hundreds digit</u>, $10y =$ the <u>tens digit</u>, and $z =$ the <u>units digit</u>.

• Consider the following:

M and N are positive, three-digit positive integers that have the same digits, but in reverse order. If N is subtracted from M, the resulting difference is 495. By how much do the first and last digits of M and N differ?

Answer: 5. Since M and N have the same 3 digits, but in reverse order, let's first represent each integer algebraically:

$$M = 100x + 10y + z \qquad N = 100z + 10y + x$$

> ➤ Next let's subtract the two, since the question asks us about **the difference of M and N**:

$$\begin{array}{r} 100x + 10y + z \\ -(100z + 10y + x) \\ \hline 99x + 0y - 99z \ \rightarrow \ 99(x - z) \end{array}$$

• According to our Algebra, $M - N = 99(x - z)$. According to the problem, however, the difference between M and N is 495. Thus, the two differences must be equal:

$$99(x - z) = 495$$

• Dividing both sides of the equation by 99 shows us that $x - z = 5$. As such, the answer to this numeric entry question must be 5, since x and z represent the first and last digits of M and N.

> ➤ To confirm the answer, choose a pair of three-digit integers with the same digits, but in reverse order.

• As long as the first and last digits differ by 5, you'll notice that no matter what numbers you choose, their difference will always be 495:

853	914	782	641
− 358	− 419	− 287	− 146
495	495	495	495

(11) Converting Repeating Decimals to Fractions – Any decimal whose digits repeat in a fixed pattern without end is known as a repeating decimal.

- For example, the decimal 0.343434… is considered a REPEATING decimal, since 0.343434… contains an infinite repetition of the digits 3 and 4.

  ➢ Conversely, numbers such as $\sqrt{2}$ = 1.4142173095+ and π = 3.14159265+ are NOT considered repeating decimals.

- Even though $\sqrt{2}$ and π both contain an infinite series of digits, neither series contains a FIXED pattern of digits that repeats without end.

- By convention, a horizontal line is placed above the repeated digits of a repeating decimal:

$$0.\overline{3} = 0.333... \qquad 0.\overline{16} = 0.1616... \qquad 0.00\overline{12} = 0.001212...$$

  ➢ On rare occasions, decimal questions can ask you to convert a repeating decimal to a fraction. Here's an example:

What is the fractional equivalent of $0.\overline{27}$?

- One way to answer such questions is to set the repeating decimal equal to x and then to MULTIPLY both sides of the equation by a POWER of 10.

  ➢ The number of ZEROES in the power of ten should equal the number of DIGITS that repeat.

- For example, in the problem above, we can first let $x = 0.\overline{27}$.

- Because $0.\overline{27}$ has TWO digits that repeat, we must then multiply both sides of the equation by 100, since 100 has TWO zeroes:

$$x = 0.\overline{27} \quad \rightarrow \quad 100x = 27.\overline{27}$$

  ➢ Once established, you can then SUBTRACT this equation from the original equation for x to eliminate the repeating decimals:

$$\begin{array}{r} 100x = 27.\overline{27} \\ - \quad x = 0.\overline{27} \\ \hline 99x = 27 \end{array}$$

- Here, $x = \dfrac{3}{11}$, since $99x = 27 \quad \rightarrow \quad x = \dfrac{27}{99} \quad \rightarrow \quad x = \dfrac{9(3)}{9(11)} = \dfrac{3}{11}$.

> ➤ To ensure that you've got it, let's work through another sample question together.

- Consider the following:

What fraction is equal to $0.\overline{018}$?

[   ]

Answer: $\frac{2}{111}$. To start, let $x = 0.\overline{018}$. Because $0.\overline{018}$ has THREE digits that repeat, we need to multiply both sides of the equation by 1,000, since 1,000 has THREE zeroes:

$$x = 0.\overline{018} \ \rightarrow \ 1,000x = 18.\overline{018}$$

> ➤ Next, let's SUBTRACT the two equations as follows to eliminate the repeating decimals:

$$\begin{array}{r} 1,000x = 18.\overline{018} \\ -\quad x = \ \ 0.\overline{018} \\ \hline 999x = 18 \end{array}$$

- Thus, $x = \frac{2}{111}$, since:

$$999x = 18 \ \rightarrow \ x = \frac{18}{999} \ \rightarrow \ x = \frac{9(2)}{9(111)} = \frac{2}{111}$$

> ➤ An even FASTER way to convert repeating decimals to fractions is to place the repeating digits over a series of NINES.

- **The number of NINES should equal the number of DIGITS that repeat.** For example:

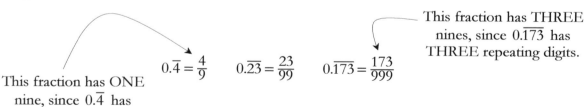

This fraction has ONE nine, since $0.\overline{4}$ has ONE repeating digit.

$$0.\overline{4} = \frac{4}{9} \qquad 0.\overline{23} = \frac{23}{99} \qquad 0.\overline{173} = \frac{173}{999}$$

This fraction has THREE nines, since $0.\overline{173}$ has THREE repeating digits.

- Thus, if $x = 1.\overline{12}$, then the fractional equivalent of x is $\frac{37}{33}$, since $1.\overline{12} = 1 + 0.\overline{12}$, and placing the TWO repeating digits over TWO nines gives us:

$$x = 1.\overline{12} = 1 + \frac{12}{99} = 1 + \frac{3(4)}{3(33)} = 1 + \frac{4}{33} = \frac{37}{33}$$

Practice Questions

(12) Problem Sets – The following questions have been arranged into three groups: fundamental, intermediate, and rare or advanced.

• Whether you're aiming for a perfect score or a score closer to average, mastery of the concepts in the FUNDAMENTAL questions is absolutely essential.

➢ As you might expect, the INTERMEDIATE questions are more difficult but are essential for test-takers who need an above-average score or higher.

• Finally, the RARE or ADVANCED questions test concepts that are very sophisticated or seldom encountered on the GRE. Mastery of such questions is required only if you need a math score above the 90th percentile.

• As always, if you find yourself confused, bogged down with busy work, or stuck, don't be afraid to fall back on your "Plan B" strategies!

➢ Remember, the "right way" to solve a problem is not always the fastest way, or the smartest.

Fundamental

	Quantity A	Quantity B
1.	$\frac{5}{3} \times 0.60$	1

2. What is 0.514659 rounded to the nearest thousandth?

(A) 0.51 (B) 0.514 (C) 0.515 (D) 0.5146 (E) 0.5147

$1{,}243 \times 10^{k}$ equals a number between 0.1 and 1

	Quantity A	Quantity B
3.	The value of integer k	–4

4. The expression $\dfrac{51.39 \times (0.997)^4}{0.02489 \div 10^{-3}}$ is approximately equal to?

    (A) 0.02   (B) 0.2   (C) 2   (D) 20   (E) 200

5. Which of the following inequalities are true?

    Select all that apply.

    $\boxed{A}$ $0 < \dfrac{1}{11} < 0.09$ $\boxed{B}$ $0 < \dfrac{1}{9} < 0.12$ $\boxed{C}$ $0.1 < \dfrac{1}{8} < 0.15$ $\boxed{D}$ $0.15 < \dfrac{1}{7} < 0.18$

6. Which of the following is equal to 36,000,000?

    (A) 36×10^7
    (B) 3.6×10^{-7}
    (C) $(3 \times 10^6) + (6 \times 10^5)$
    (D) $(30 \times 10^{-7}) + (6 \times 10^{-6})$
    (E) $(3 \times 10^7) + (6 \times 10^6)$

7. Which of the following is most nearly equal to $\sqrt{8} \div 2$?

    (A) $\dfrac{6}{5}$ (B) $\dfrac{5}{4}$ (C) $\dfrac{4}{3}$ (D) $\dfrac{7}{5}$ (E) $\dfrac{3}{2}$

	Quantity A	Quantity B
8.	100,000,000	9^8

9. If k is an integer and 0.0020301×10^k is greater than 1,000, what is the least possible value of k?

    (A) 2   (B) 3   (C) 4   (D) 5   (E) 6

$b = 4.16894$ and $\boxed{b}$ is the decimal expression for b rounded to the nearest thousandth.

	Quantity A	Quantity B
10.	The number of decimal places where b and $\boxed{b}$ differ	3

Intermediate

11. How many 2-digit positive integers are there such that the product of their two digits is 18?

(A) One (B) Two (C) Four (D) Six (E) Eight

$$r = 0.12\overset{3}{\cancel{5}}8$$

Digit s denotes the thousandths digit in the decimal representation of r above. If r were rounded to the nearest thousandth, the result would be 0.124.

	Quantity A	Quantity B
12.	The value of digit s	4

13. A certain accountant mistakenly divided a number by 115 instead of 1.15, resulting in an incorrect quotient. Which of the following is a single operation that the accountant could type into his calculator to fix the error?

Indicate all such operations.

A Multiply by 100   B Divide by 100   C Multiply by 0.01   D Divide by 0.01

x and y are both greater than 0 and less than 1.

	Quantity A	Quantity B
14.	$x^2 + y^2$	$x + y$

15. If $x = 0.\overline{8}$, $y = \sqrt{0.\overline{8}}$, and $z = (0.\overline{8})^2$, then which of the following must be true?

(A) $x < y < z$ (B) $x < z < y$ (C) $y < x < z$ (D) $y < z < x$ (E) $z < x < y$

	Quantity A	Quantity B
16.	0.00012×0.00012	1.44×10^{-8}

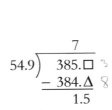

$$54.9 \overline{)\ 385.\Box}$$
$$\underline{-\ 384.\Delta}$$
$$1.5$$

17. If the solution of the division problem above is correct, which digit does □ represent?

(A) 0   (B) 2   (C) 3   (D) 5   (E) 8

m is a digit in the decimal 2.4*m*5, and 2.4*m*5 is less than 2.43.

Quantity A	Quantity B
18. *m*	1

19. If $a = (0.77777)^2$, $b = \dfrac{1}{(0.77777)^2}$, and $c = (1 - 0.77777)^2 - 1$, which of the following must be true?

(A) $a < b < c$ (B) $b < c < a$ (C) $c < a < b$ (D) $b < a < c$ (E) $a < c < b$

Quantity A	Quantity B
20. $\dfrac{(0.0009)(0.035)}{(0.002)(0.05)(0.007)}$	$\dfrac{(0.00036)(0.0045)}{(0.006)(0.005)(0.009)}$

21. If $x = \dfrac{5.1 \times 10^{-4}}{0.00000017 \div 10^{-3}}$, what is the value of *x*?

$$\boxed{3}$$

In a certain two-digit number, the units digit is half the tens digit.

Quantity A	Quantity B
22. The units digit	5

Last year, state *S* had a total expenditure of 3.6×10^9
and a population of 0.72 million.

Quantity A	Quantity B
23. The per capita expenditure of state *S*	$4,980

Rare or Advanced

24. If a two-digit positive integer has its digits reversed, the resulting integer differs from the original by 36. By how much do the two digits differ?

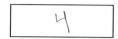

$$s = 25^3 \times 34^3 \times 43^3$$

Quantity A	Quantity B
25. The units digit of s	0

26. The number 0.01 is how many times as great as the number $(0.01)^4$?

(A) 10^2 (B) 10^4 (C) 10^6 (D) 10^8 (E) 10^{10}

$$n = 98,765 \times 11,111$$

Quantity A	Quantity B
27. The units digit of n	The tens digit of n

28. In the repeating decimal $0.\overline{25138}$, the 27th digit to the right of the decimal point is

(A) 1   (B) 2   (C) 3   (D) 5   (E) 8

29. If $x = 0.\overline{054}$, what is the smallest fractional equivalent of x?

$$\frac{27}{500}$$

Quantity A	Quantity B
30. The value of the units digit in 6^{99}	The value of the units digit in 9^{66}

(13) Solutions – Video solutions for each of the previous questions can be found on our website at **www.sherpaprep.com/videos**.

• BOOKMARK this address for future visits!

  ➤ To view the videos, you'll need the LOGIN and PASSWORD that you created upon registering your copy of Arithmetic & "Plan B" Strategies.

• If you have yet to register your book yet, please go to **www.sherpaprep.com/activate** and enter your email address, last name, and shipping address.

• Be sure to provide the SAME last name and shipping address that you used to purchase your copy of Master Key to the GRE or to enroll in your GRE course with Sherpa Prep!

  ➤ When checking your answers, we encourage you to watch the solution for any problem that you answered INCORRECTLY

• The same goes for any problem that took you MORE than TWO MINUTES to solve.

• After digesting the explanation, REVISIT your mistake a couple of days later to ensure that the problem no longer poses issues to you.

  ➤ If you struggle to solve the problem a SECOND time, add it to your "LOG of ERRORS" and redo it every few weeks.

• Solving tricky questions MORE THAN ONCE is the best way to learn from your mistakes and to avoid similar difficulties on your actual exam.

Fundamental	Intermediate		Rare or Advanced
1. C	11. C	21. 3	24. 4
2. C	12. B	22. B	25. C
3. C	13. A, D	23. A	26. C
4. C	14. B		27. A
5. B, C	15. E		28. D
6. E	16. C		29. 2/37
7. D	17. E		30. A
8. A	18. D		
9. E	19. C		
10. C	20. A		

Sherpa Prep

Master Key to the GRE

Have an iPhone or iPad?
Get the App!

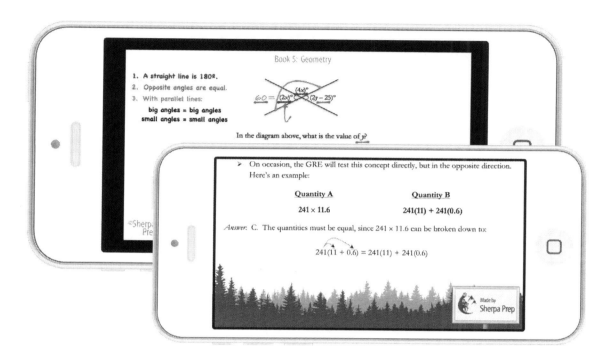

© **GRE Math by Sherpa Prep**

Study on the Go!

- ☑ Watch Videos
- ☑ Make Study Lists
- ☑ Take Practice Quizzes
- ☑ Analyze Stats
- ☑ Create Error Logs

Available Now @ the Apple App Store

Notes

Notes

Notes

Notes

Notes

Notes